# After the Celtic Tiger

## Challenges Ahead

THE O'BRIEN PRESS

DUBLIN

# THE AUTHORS

**J. Peter Clinch** is Director of Graduate Studies at the Department of Environmental Studies, University College Dublin. He has Bachelor's and Master's degrees in economics and a PhD in environmental economics. Prior to taking up his present post, he was a Research Fellow in the Department of Economics at UCD. He recently held a visiting position at the University of California, Berkeley. Peter Clinch has also worked as a consultant for, *inter alia*, the World Bank, the Overseas Development Administration, the OECD and the European Union. He has written extensively on the interface between the economy and the environment and has published work on most areas of environmental economics and policy in books and international academic journals. He has a particular interest in European Union environmental policy and his most recent research examines the impact of rapid economic growth on the sustainability of natural environments.

**Frank Convery** is Heritage Trust Professor of Environmental Studies at University College Dublin. He was educated at UCD and the State University of New York and has degrees in forestry and resource economics. Prior to taking up his post at UCD, he was Assistant and then Associate Professor of Natural Resource Economics at Duke University, USA, and Research Professor at the Economic and Social Research Institute, Ireland. Frank Convery is active on a number of EU-wide investigations and bodies, including membership of the Science Committee of the European Environment Agency. He has written extensively on resource and environmental economics issues with particular reference to agriculture, forestry, energy, minerals, land use, urbanisation, environment and development in developing countries. At present, his research relates to European Union Environmental Policy with particular reference to the use, potential and effectiveness of market-based instruments.

 **Brendan Walsh** has been Professor of National Economics at University College Dublin since 1980. He graduated from UCD in 1961, obtained a doctorate in economics from Boston College in 1966 and taught at the University of Massachusetts and Tufts University before returning to Ireland to take up a post at the Economic and Social Research Institute in 1969. He has served overseas as an economic advisor with the Harvard Institute for International Development – in Iran in 1975-76 and in The Gambia in 1989-91. He has also served as a consultant with the World Bank, the OECD and the Commission of the EU. He has written widely on the Irish economy in academic journals and his textbook with Anthony Leddin, *The Macroeconomy of Ireland*, is now in its fourth edition. His most recent research has examined the effects of breaking the sterling link on the Irish pound – a topic that is relevant to the impact of the euro on the Irish economy. He is a member of the Royal Irish Academy.

First published 2002 by The O'Brien Press Ltd.,
20 Victoria Road, Dublin 6, Ireland.
Tel: +353 1 4923333; Fax: +353 1 4922777
e-mail: books@obrien.ie
Website: www.obrien.ie


ISBN 0-86278-767-X

British Library Cataloguing-in-publication Data
A catalogue reference for this title is available from the British Library.

1 2 3 4 5 6 7 8 9 10
02 03 04 05 06 07 08 09 10


Typesetting, design, layout: The O'Brien Press Ltd.
Cover separations: C&A Print Services Ltd.
Printing: Omnia Books Ltd.

# Contents

# Acknowledgements

There is a theory about universities, that they are places where reflection on the great issues of life is facilitated and encouraged, where intellectual freedom is absolute, and where the unthinkable can be thought, all in a measured and collegial atmosphere. The reality is often very different; teaching, correcting, seminars and conferences, grant hunting, seeking the holy grail of refereed publications, committee and faculty meetings, gossip and low and high politics – all conspire to reduce serious reflection to a few moments in the shower on a Monday morning.

For all that, we are grateful to our employer and our *alma mater*, University College Dublin, for giving us the space, the context and the opportunity to think about where we've been and where we are going, to facilitate our coming together, and for guaranteeing us the freedom to say what we think. We are also grateful to colleagues and participants at numerous conferences and seminars who with their own presentations and feedback to ours have informed our views.

Recent events have punctured for ever the illusion that all our politicians and public servants are incorruptible paragons of virtue. But while venality, thievery, gombeenism and narrow self-interest are manifest, it is clear to us that Ireland's achievements over the past decades would not have been possible without the consistent input of many politicians and public servants who opted in the main for what was best for the country. Excellence will not prevail if it is not fostered at the political level. The challenges we identify will require political integrity and skills of the highest order in the future. We hope that the current malaise will not discourage those of talent from engaging in politics and the public service.

We are grateful to our families for indulging the eccentric time-keeping and peculiar obsessions that writing even a modest volume entails, and to the staff of O'Brien Press for the professionalism, care, attention and speed with which they handled this project.

Finally, we are grateful to the Business Research Unit for providing a grant that allowed this book to be produced to a higher standard and with more expedition than would have been possible in its absence.

# Preface

*'It's tough to make predictions, especially about the future.'* Yogi Berra

The year 2001 was a watershed. The 'dotcom' bubble had already burst by the middle of 2000, but the dreaded word 'recession' was not much used until people returned to work after the Christmas–New Year holiday in January 2001. Everyone now knows that the US entered a recession in the second quarter of the year; the burning issue is how deep and how long this will be. For a while we Europeans – especially we Irish – smugly believed that we were insulated from the cold winds blowing across the Atlantic. But gradually the truth dawned – the US is the locomotive that pulled the world economy through the boom of the 1990s and when that locomotive began to slow, Europe and Ireland slowed too. As the year wore on commentators in Ireland began to notice that the optimistic projects on which Finance Minister Charlie McCreevy had based his budget of December 2000 were more like pulp fiction than sober economic forecasts.

And then there was 11 September 2001. W.B. Yeats's familiar words come to mind: 'All changed, changed utterly. A terrible beauty is born.'

How terrible remains to be seen. But the event does remind us that history is always a surprise, and the best predictions of economists are often interesting but usually wrong. As has been said: 'An economic forecaster is like a cross-eyed javelin thrower; he doesn't win many accuracy contests, but he keeps the crowd's attention.'

So, in this book we do not propose to make forecasts. For the past decade, the global economic tide has been coming in and the Irish boat has risen with it. But the Irish achievement has not merely been that the country sat passively on automatic pilot while global forces did the rest. First, we did not resist the rising tide, as we did in the 1950s. During that melancholy (for Ireland) decade, as the global economy expanded around us, with the best of intentions we busied ourselves throwing heavy rocks into the hold, ensuring that mass emigration and poverty would be our lot. Ireland learned then that aiming for economic self-sufficiency is the road to nowhere. Over the past two decades we adopted a more positive attitude and actively piloted our economy in ways that ensured that our speed and progress made maximum use of the favourable circumstances facing us. And this in turn spawned a cottage industry to which some of us have contributed, explaining to the world how the 'Irish economic miracle' happened, and what lessons there might be for other countries.

But now the global economic tide is ebbing. How far and for how long no one can say, but it is clear that the heady years of the 1990s are over. How can Ireland steer the economic ship so that its retreat is not destructive? As important, how can the economy ensure that it quickly rises and recovers momentum when the tide finally turns?

In *Managing Crises Before They Happen* Ian Mitroff insists that companies need to develop crisis management capabilities rather than crisis management plans.[1] Plans deal with known or foreseen dangers, e.g. food contamination in the food industry, fire and explosions in the chemical industry. Crisis management is the capability to deal with the completely unexpected, to prepare for the unthinkable before its occurrence. Samuel Beckett's mordant comment, 'Death has not required us to keep a day free,' reminds us of the ultimate futility of being too inclusive in our planning. The emphasis on management capabilities rather than 'a plan' seems to be particularly germane at this time – because undoubtedly other surprises await. In this book we focus on some adaptive capabilities that should be fostered in Ireland to cope with the current adversity. We want to identify not just the difficulties but also the challenges and opportunities to which such adversity gives rise.

And we as a people have experienced adversity in the past, and can learn from that. As a country we survived mass starvation in the nineteenth century, while the twentieth century brought a rising, a war of independence and a civil war that resulted in the extirpation of a whole generation of leaders, a depression and an 'economic war' with our most important trading partner in the 1930s, a traumatic and largely self-induced economic and social haemorrhage in the 1950s and another severe recession in the 1980s. And still there was enough vitality, good luck and creativity to make Ireland the fastest-growing economy in Europe in the 1990s.

We are assuming here that the global economy will slow down significantly. Given such adversity, how should Ireland respond? We offer a few big ideas. First, learn from what has worked in the past. This may seem trite and self-evident, but when stresses appear it is all too easy to ignore the lessons of history. Falkland's advice is sound: 'When change is not necessary, it is necessary not to change.'

Second, maintain investment. This means keeping faith with future generations by providing the capacity in education, transport, housing and so on that will be needed. And this is difficult, because as growth slows maintaining investment is more painful in terms of forgone consumption than it is during boom times.

Third, encourage and facilitate innovation and quality. In an analysis of Research and Development (R&D) expenditure in the UK, the Department of Trade and Industry notes that in previous business downturns, companies that have cut R&D investment have often found that their range of products and services compare less well with competitors when the upturn comes and it is then more difficult to protect market share and value added.[2] And countries that score well in the Summary Innovation Index (SII) – based on tertiary education, business investment, home internet access (where the US leads), numbers of new science and engineering graduates, state-funded R&D and information and communication technology investments (where Europe and Japan lead) – have managed to increase innovation performance and reduce poverty, and there is a strong positive correlation between the SII and the index of environmental sustainability. Highly innovative countries tend to give high priority to sustainability.

Artists observe and then interpret, using the wellsprings of their imaginations to give new meaning to old ideas and images. And in doing so, they can make us laugh, increase our self-awareness, stretch our understanding of ourselves and life about us.

We authors lack the talent to make the artist's imaginative leap. But we do think we can help make sense of the economic and social forces we observe in Ireland, to bring whatever insights we have to the marketplace where 'things are done' – a sort of response to Seamus Deane's plea:

> I remember at times
> How irresponsible I have
> Become. No ruling passion
> Obsesses me, although passions
> Are what I play among.
> I'll know the library in a city
> Before I know there is a slum.
> I could wish the weight of
> Learning would bring me down
> To where things are done.

Ireland has had a great economic run: unprecedented economic growth lasting for nearly a decade, higher incomes, more jobs, more people, more variety. For over ten years it seems as if everything has gone right, both externally and internally. But just as everything can go right, everything can also go wrong. Murphy's Law still waits in the wings to exert its sobering influence.

In any event, the growth couldn't go on now as it had. Some of the factors that made it possible, especially the rapid growth in the labour force, are disappearing, the US recession casts its shadow and the exchange rate and other factors are likely to be less favourable in the future than they have been. In addition, the costs of rapid and sustained growth – more physical and visible pollution, more congestion, and high costs of accommodation – are still manifest and harder to deal with when less new wealth is being generated.

We started this book at a time when the concern was with 'overheating' – the notion that the economy was growing so fast that it would inevitably suffer a 'hard landing'. This fear was quickly replaced by a more immediate concern as the sudden downturn in the economy became evident. As the year 2001 wore on, the evidence accumulated that the boom was giving way to something less attractive. This demanded that we focus on how to adjust to adversity in the short run as well as taking a longer-term view of our economic prospects.

So the purpose of this book is to explore what has happened but, more particularly, to look to the future and begin to paint a strategy of adjustment so that shocks and reverses can be absorbed without lasting damage. We start with a review of Ireland's recent economic progress, why it occurred and why it is unlikely to continue. We then turn our attention to a range of specific themes and forces. We argue that how we react to, and deal with, these issues will determine our success at adjusting to adversity. The issues we've chosen to tackle are: the boom and its aftermath and the importance of productivity, globalisation and free trade, population growth and immigration, wage and tax policies and the partnership processes that mediate them, unaffordable/affordable housing, traffic congestion (and the spatial policies that shape their location and character), resource management and environmental quality, and quality of life generally.

A year is a very long time in economics! The concern that the Irish economy was growing 'too fast' has changed to the more elemental fear of a return to recession, stagnant living standards, falling output, rising unemployment and a resumption of emigration. Without abandoning our exploration of longterm economic and environmental issues, we have rebalanced our book to include a discussion of the appropriate response to the current cyclical downturn and a discussion of the strategy that will quickly restore an acceptable rate of economic growth.

# CHAPTER 1

# Our Approach

We are economists. And economists have a certain perspective that shapes their world view. We accept that this is not the only view – see box p.18 – but it is useful for the reader to understand where we're coming from. Many of these ideas are not popularly accepted but we hope that a sympathy will grow for our point of view as one chapter follows the next. To help readers adjust to our jargon we include a 'glossary of terms' at the back of the book.

These are the fundamental elements of our perspective:

**Prices are important**: We believe that if something is given away free, it is likely to be wasted. And the higher the price, the more likely it is that the good or service will be used parsimoniously.

**Sunk costs – costs already incurred – should be irrelevant in making decisions**: This is a pedantic way of saying don't throw good money after bad. If costs already incurred are irrelevant, the implication is that we are more interested in the future than the past. And this has profound implications. Reflecting on the southern US, William Faulkner observed: 'The past isn't dead and gone. It isn't even past yet.' We believe that the fascination with the past as a shaper of tomorrow can be profoundly destructive, and nowhere more than in Northern Ireland. But, of course, a focus on the future has its own dangers.

## PROFESSIONAL IMPERATIVES

George Bernard Shaw defined a profession as a 'conspiracy against the laity.' We agree. This largely unconscious conspiracy has two strands. First, professions attempt to make their knowledge impenetrable to the rest of us by using acronyms and jargon that simultaneously intimidates, confuses and impresses. Secondly, every profession has a central idea, what the French call an *'idée fixe'* which determines the decision they make when a problem or challenge arises. And so the profession predetermines the decision. This professional reflex is often unconscious, but no less real for that. Engineers build. Faced with serious traffic congestion, an engineer will propose a structural solution: build a light rail system, widen the road, build a bypass. Planners love coloured maps; they zone the problem out of existence. The big idea of lawyers is laws and regulations. For foresters, planting trees is the response; faced with a flooding problem they will suggest that trees be planted in the uplands; faced with an outbreak of syphilis, they may even suggest that trees be planted to distract the potentially afflicted with sylvan beauty! Ecologists will argue that interfering with natural processes will make matters worse for posterity and that no action is the right action. For architects, design is the solution: urban dysfunction is a product of poor urban design.

Ivan Illich has gone further and argued that professions are part of a 'reciprocity principle' whereby they have a vested interest in dysfunction – teachers in ignorance, police in crime, environmental managers in environmental degradation, economists in economic disarray.

For economists, the *idée fixe* is the efficacy of the market, which we view as something of a panacea. Faced with traffic congestion, the economic analysis argues that the fundamental problem is that there is no price signal faced by road users that rations road space such that demand and supply are brought into equilibrium. Forget about new engineering solutions, new laws, or zoning. Use electronic road pricing, and fix a price for its use at a level that allows traffic to flow.

**Markets are powerful forces for meeting our needs**: As a species, it is the propensity to trade that is perhaps our most characteristic feature. Adam Smith observed: 'Man is the only animal that makes bargains; one dog does not exchange bones with another dog.' And the appeal to others' self-interest as a source of our own well-being is captured in what is perhaps the most frequently quoted statement in the field of economics, from Smith's *The Wealth of Nations* (1776):

> It is not from the benevolence of the butcher, the brewer, or the baker that we expect our dinner, but from their regard to their own interest. We address ourselves not to their humanity but their self love, and never talk to them of our necessities but of their advantages.

**But markets sometimes fail to deliver on their promise to advance well-being**: Contrary to popular opinion, economists are not uncritical of the market system. The market system is subject to flaws and abuse. Sometimes markets are not competitive, and where this is the case consumers will suffer a combination of higher prices and lower quality. And Adam Smith saw the tendency to collude as ubiquitous: 'People of the same trade seldom meet together, even for merriment and diversion, but the conversation ends in a conspiracy against the public, or in some contrivance to raise prices.' When monopoly power is contrived or created, this generates what economists call 'rent seekers' – individuals or companies attempting to get a share of the excess profits that such monopoly confers. Here rent signifies not the normal profit yielded in competitive markets, but the additional surplus yielded by some combination of market power and insider knowledge. There is an Irish word *'gaimbín'*, meaning usurer, which has transferred to English as 'gombeen' or 'gombeen man' – the local rent seeker, exploiting position, power and knowledge to advantage. And many of the accusations arising in the recent tribunals – re-zoning of land, securing of exclusive telecommunication licences – are examples of rent seeking.

Furthermore, markets cannot work when property rights are not assigned, and this occurs across a range of resources and environments. Thus, marine fisheries everywhere are being destroyed because access is free and unlimited, and our technological capacity to find, to catch and to store fish has increased a thousand-fold. The global commons, such as the upper atmosphere and the reservoirs of biodiversity, are under increasing pressure because access has been free. And water quality is deteriorating in Ireland for the same reason: there is no real charge for using waterways as sinks for disposing of waste.

**Resources are finite – how and for what we allocate resources defines our priorities**: No matter how wealthy humans become, there will never be enough resources to meet our desires. Earlier we noted that our species is unique in its propensity to trade. We also are unique in the infinity of our desires. Most people feel that more income and more wealth is better than less, and this seems to apply with particular force to those who already have most. Of course, this is not a universal trait. Some religions, including strands of Christianity and Buddhism, extol the inherent merits of frugality and the idea of the minimum as the optimum. But practice lags behind promise in this regard.

Culture and values are crucial determinants of priorities. For example, it is often averred that Irish people put a very high priority on the value of educating their children. Many families have made and continue to make enormous sacrifices to ensure that their children get 'the best start' possible educationally. And in some cases, expenditure on housing, holidays, food etc. are all constrained in order to meet this over-riding imperative. To the extent that this is a cultural imperative, it is, of course, very valuable for society as it results in an improved overall level of education which benefits everybody.

Linked to this is the concept that economists call 'opportunity costs' – what is inevitably foregone elsewhere if we devote increased resources to an area. Which is to say that if we expand public expenditure in one area, we will either have to increase taxes, thus reducing the share of income being retained privately, or reduce public expenditure in some other area. There are no 'free lunches'. Implicit in the choices made is the concept of benefits and costs. If we expand expenditure on primary education, and this is financed by reducing expenditure on, say, public housing, this implies that we feel that the added benefits resulting from additional expenditure on education are greater than the resulting reduction in benefits from public housing. Nothing is free.

**Taxes have hidden costs**: People look to the public sector to provide them with certain public services and these have to be paid for by taxation. There is a hidden cost in raising most taxes: higher taxes distort people's behaviour. They affect the choices made between things that are taxed and things that are not taxed. An income tax, for example, discourages work; a (high) tax on coffee could encourage some of us to drink beer. So we should raise an extra euro in taxation only if we can be sure that the benefits yielded exceed not just the money raised but also the cost of raising it.

**Adaptability and innovation**: Because change is inevitable, it follows that people and cultures that can adapt rapidly to changed circumstances will be more successful than those that do not. It is one of the many conceits of the current middle-aged generation that we are uniquely assaulted with rapid change. But our ancestors dealt with the horrors of frequent and endemic famine in the nineteenth century; early in the twentieth century they coped with the arrival of electricity, phones, trams and cars. In the thirties, the collapse of world economies resulted in sustained and impoverishing unemployment, the fifties saw tragedy visited on hundreds of thousands as a result of a (self-imposed) protectionist policy. And so adaptation to extreme events and new technologies is a routine and predictable part of the human experience. But how we organise our affairs can influence the speed and appropriateness of the adaptive process. And cultural reflexes are important. Those who anticipate opportunities in adversity are likely to find them. In sailing, they say that races are won at night, in light winds. When the economic winds have slackened is the time that companies with the right stuff show their mettle.

**Policy instruments:** Policy analysts talk of 'policy instruments' as if there were a tool box from which whatever instruments were needed to fix a problem could be taken and applied. What we mean by such instruments are the types of policy interventions that can be used to change outcomes. These include:

➤ *Regulation or command and control*, where government decides what is or is not acceptable, and passes a law or regulation that must be complied with.

➤ *Tax incentives and charges*, which can either provide tax breaks to encourage particular forms of activity, or impose taxes or charges on activity, e.g. pollution, that are judged to be damaging.

➤ *Public investment*, where government intervenes directly, or in partnership, to provide infrastructure, goods or services.

➤ *Emissions trading*, whereby quotas of emissions are given to polluters, and they are allowed to buy and sell these credits, as long as they hold credits equivalent to their emissions.

➤ *Information*, whereby producers and/or consumers are provided with systematic information that helps improve decisions.

➤ *Voluntary agreements*, whereby either firms meeting some government-specified environmental or other target qualify for tax or other exemptions, or groups of firms agree to meet a collective target.

➤ *Fiscal policy*, whereby aggregate public expenditure and taxation are adjusted up or down to either stimulate economic activity or constrain both economic activity and inflation.

➤ *Monetary policy*, whereby interest rates are adjusted up or down by changes in the money supply. (This option is no longer available in Ireland as it is now in the eurozone.)

**Marginality – looking at incremental changes**: Economics is more effective as an analytical framework when changes at the margin are relatively modest. This reflects the philosophy of Cardinal John Henry Newman, the founding president of our own college, University College Dublin:

> I do not ask to see
> The distant scene; one step enough for me.
>
> (Lead Kindly Light)

**Income distribution and fairness**: Economists are not renowned for the attention they pay to the distribution of income, particularly to the losers in the processes of change. This is, in part, because utility – the value individuals get from consumption – and equity are difficult to quantify definitively and fit into models of behaviour. We feel that this dimension is important both on its own merits, and also because unless choices and processes are felt by most people to be reasonable and fair, they will run into political difficulties and implementation will fail.

**Quality of life**: It is often perceived that economists are not interested in non-monetary things. However, we recognise that there are lots of aspects of life that are not bought and sold in markets, and therefore do not have a price, yet are of great value. The satisfaction people feel with life depends on much more than the size of their bank account or wage packet. It also depends on such things as their health, relationships and family life, and the natural and built environment that surrounds them.

# CHAPTER 2

# The Boom and Its Aftermath

The Irish boom of the 1990s was like receiving an unexpected but welcome baby. We woke up one morning and there it was on the doorstep. For years, analysts had been trying to explain why Ireland's economic performance was so lacklustre when all around us prospered. The National Economic and Social Council commissioned reports about it.[1] Then suddenly, all changed. But some refused to believe change had occurred. Some of our own academic colleagues argued that the recorded growth was a chimera, a statistical delusion caused by the way multinationals over-price their outputs to take advantage of Ireland's relatively low corporate tax rates. The effects on the well-being of the population, as judged by conventional indicators, are documented below; and in later chapters we discuss a range of environmental and quality-of-life issues. The national self-image has been transformed. Ireland has gone from being a country to get out of to a country to get into. The melancholia reflected in the emigrant songs, like Andy Irvine's 'It's a long long way from Clare to here', are like echoes from a distant age. Ireland is finally delivering on Sean Lemass's insight that making our own patch worth joining was likely to be a more convincing strategy as regards Northern Ireland than bombing and knee-capping.

In this chapter we look at the miracle years of the 'Celtic Tiger' and ask what happened and why. We are talking about the 1990s, defined (correctly) to end on 31 December 2000. And indeed it was in the weeks after this that the world began to move, and Ireland with it, towards a period of slower growth.

We report a consensus view of the forces behind the Irish boom.[2] We then look at the deterioration in Irish economic prospects that occurred in the course of 2001 and ask what can be done to minimise the fall in our growth rate.

## The Record

Between 1993 and 2001 the annual real growth rate of the Irish economy has been more than double the average recorded over the previous three decades – 8% compared with 3.5%. Figure 1 shows the Irish and EU growth rates. Although the use of GDP is a limited measure of the 'true' performance of the Irish economy, there is no doubt that throughout the 1990s Ireland significantly outperformed all other EU countries.

The performance of the labour market has been even more remarkable. The numbers at work have risen by 45% over the past twelve years, representing an annual average increase of over 3% a year. In contrast, over this period there was little net employment growth in the EU (Figure 2) and employment in the US increased by 'only' about 1% a year.

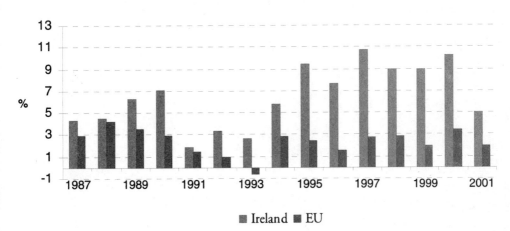

■ Ireland ■ EU

Figure 1: GDP GROWTH, 1987–2001

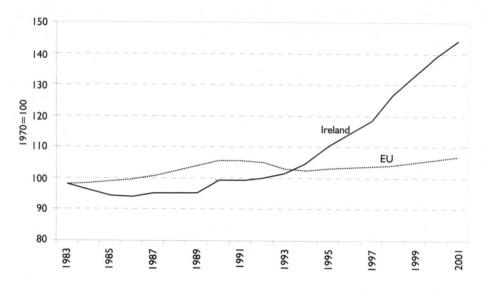

Figure 2: EMPLOYMENT IN IRELAND AND THE EU, 1983–2001

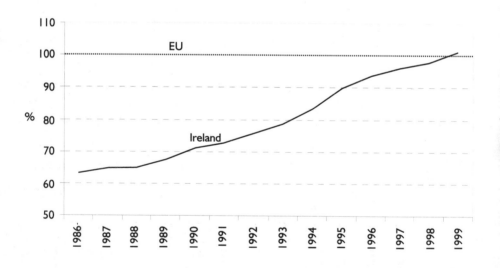

Figure 3: IRISH STANDARD OF LIVING RELATIVE TO THE EU, 1986–1999

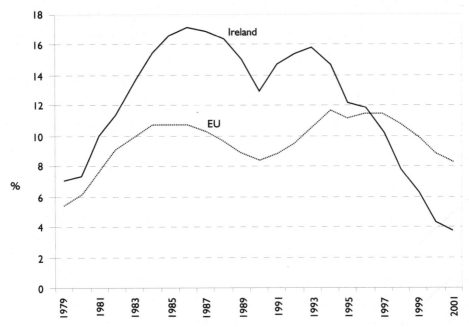

Figure 4: IRISH AND EU UNEMPLOYMENT RATES, 1979–2001

This boom accomplished many things:

➤ Rapid growth of GDP per person moved Ireland up the EU living-standards league table. Having long endured a standard of living that was only two-thirds of the EU average, Ireland has now risen to the European average in terms of GDP per person, adjusted for the purchasing power of currencies (Figure 3).

➤ The unemployment rate fell from a peak of 17% in the 1980s to under 4% in 2001 (Figure 4).

➤ Women's labour-force participation rate rose from its low initial level to close to the EU average.

➤ The high net emigration rate of the 1980s was replaced by what is now the highest net immigration rate in the EU. For the first time in modern history Ireland is witnessing the growth of communities of residents who have no previous links with the country.

27

The boom was exceptional, not just by historical Irish standards but also in an international perspective. Apart from the 'Asian Tigers' between 1960 and 1990, and China since 1978, no other countries have sustained such rapid growth for a comparable length of time. In light of the sharp reversal of the boom in Asia in the late 1990s, and the subsequent uneven recovery, fears were naturally expressed about the possibility of a hard landing for the Irish economy. But let us not lose sight of the fact that after the crash these economies remain prosperous and successful, and several countries – Malaysia, for example – recovered quickly. However, the example of Singapore is more alarming, due to the very sharp recession it experienced.

In the 1980s Irish living standards were a long way behind the EU average and the employment/population ratio was very low. These considerations help explain why the country improved so rapidly: there was a lot of ground to be made up. Economic historians have been puzzled by why the Irish economy failed to grow as rapidly as several poorer European economies over the immediate post-war period – Italy, for example. Instead of asking: Why did the Irish economy suddenly begin to catch up in the 1990s, we could ask: Why did Ireland lag behind for so long? The answer is that bad economic policies – the continuation of protectionist trade policies into the late 1950s and irresponsible fiscal experimentation in the late 1970s – delayed Ireland's entry to the European 'convergence club'. Once the country had rectified its fiscal imbalances in the first half of the 1980s and copper-fastened its access to the market of the European Union by implementing the Single European Act in the early 1990s, it was well-positioned to attract foreign direct investment (FDI) from the booming US economy and quickly, if belatedly, catch up with the world's richest countries.

But these points do not detract from Ireland's remarkable achievement during the 1990s. They do explain why the country caught up during the 1990s. Other EU member states – Spain, Portugal, and Greece – enjoyed living standards comparable with Ireland's in the 1980s but fell significantly behind during the 1990s. These 'Cohesion

**BENEFITS OF 'FULL EMPLOYMENT'**

'The good news about the disadvantaged in the US is that the economic boom of the 1990s has brought a noticeable improvement in their economic well-being and social behaviour. With unemployment in the region of 4%–5% for an extended period, the earnings of low-wage workers rose; inner-city young people got jobs; the rate of crime fell; teenage births fell; the welfare caseload dropped; poverty rates fell. The 1990s showed that full employment can be a highly successful social policy.'

Richard Freeman, 'The US "Underclass" in a Booming Economy', *World Economics* 1 (2), April–June 2000

countries' benefited as Ireland did from the substantial transfers from the EU, but their growth rates are substantially lower. It is clear that funds from the EU are not the only source of our success. Further afield, New Zealand and Canada, once close to the top of the international living-standards league table, fell behind during the 1990s. There is nothing automatic about catching up or staying at the top.

## Explaining the Boom

The boom was the product of a number of interacting factors, some of them due to good domestic economic policies, others to favourable external developments. These include:

### under our control

> ➤ A favourable environment for FDI, including low corporate tax rates, and enlightened promotion of Ireland as an industrial location by the IDA
> ➤ An elastic supply of good-quality (assisted by increased investment in education from the 1960s) and relatively inexpensive labour
> ➤ Flexible labour-market practices and industrial peace
> ➤ A stable macroeconomic environment, including strong public finances and price stability.

29

**not under our control**

> ➤ Advantageous exchange rates against sterling and the US dollar
>
> ➤ The sustained US boom
>
> ➤ The impact of new IT technologies on productivity
>
> ➤ Low energy prices and reductions in the cost of access to Ireland
>
> ➤ Significant additional EU transfers for infrastructure and training.

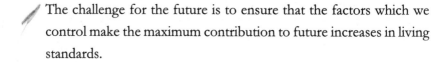 The challenge for the future is to ensure that the factors which we control make the maximum contribution to future increases in living standards.

## Unbalanced Growth?

A striking feature of Irish economic growth during the 1990s was the increasing importance of inward investment. The new FDI attracted to the country – most of it from the US – has made an enormous contribution to the economy in terms of employment, export growth and tax revenue. But the other side of that coin has been the growing dependency on a relatively narrow production base. It is estimated that between 1990 and 1999 GDP increased by 75%, but the three sectors dominated by multinational corporations (MNCs) – chemicals, computers and instrument engineering, and electrical engineering – grew by 275% and contributed some 30 points of the 75 percentage points increase in domestic production.[3] This growth pattern has clearly increased the economy's exposure to the performance of the US economy and to cyclical conditions in these three sectors. But – see box opposite– while our dependence is considerable, its overall impact and implications can be exaggerated.

**MEASURING THE CONTRIBUTION OF MULTINATIONAL CORPORATIONS (MNCS)**

'The Central Statistics Office (CSO) estimates that in 1998 the 34 largest MNCs accounted for £25 billion exports, but they imported £16 billion and their profits (net of taxes) came to £7 billion. When these and other deductions are allowed for, their contribution to a GNP of £53 billion was about £3 billion. So, while these companies accounted for over half total exports, their direct contribution to GNP was only 6%. An implication of this is that we are less exposed to the adverse effects of a US recession than an uncritical examination of the contribution of MNCs to our export boom suggests.'

William Keating, 'Measuring the Economy – Problems and Prospects', paper presented to the Statistical and Social Inquiry Society of Ireland, 26 October 2000

## The Rich Got Richer and the Poor Got ... Richer

One of the most frequent complaints about the era of the Celtic Tiger is that the poor got left behind. Many doubted the validity of President John F. Kennedy's slogan that 'a rising tide lifts all boats.' If true, the failure of the Irish economic boom to benefit the poorest and most disadvantaged in the economy would be a serious indictment. What are the facts?

The good news is that there was a dramatic fall in the level of absolute poverty in Ireland during the boom. This was the result of three forces:

> The rise in real (net of inflation) after-tax household income

> The fall in the unemployment rate from 17% to 4%

> The rise in the real value of social-welfare benefits.

Changes in poverty levels can be measured by a 'real-income standard'. This standard is the percentage of a household's income that is required to buy a certain 'basket' of goods at a particular point in time. Using this approach, it can be shown that there was a dramatic fall in

31

the proportion of the population living below a real-income standard set in 1987 and that this proportion increased in line with price inflation thereafter, as may be seen from Table 1.

**Table 1**
**Level of Absolute Poverty in Ireland, 1994–98**
**Based on a Constant Real-income Standard**

|  | 1994 | 1997 | 1998 |
|---|---|---|---|
| Proportion Falling Below 40% of Standard | 1.9 | 1.3 | 0.6 |
| Proportion Falling Below 50% of Standard | 7.0 | 2.9 | 1.6 |
| Proportion Falling Below 60% of Standard | 17.7 | 8.0 | 5.7 |

Source: *Monitoring Poverty Trends and Exploring Poverty Dynamics in Ireland*, ESRI Policy Research Series 41, June 2001

Reading across the rows of this table we see that the incidence of extreme poverty – those living below 40% of the 1987 standard – fell from 1.9% to 0.6%, while those in less extreme poverty (60% of the 1987 standard) fell from 17.7% to 5.7% of the population.

Using a different approach, another study concluded that under a variety of technical economic assumptions there was a significant rise in the welfare of the Irish population between 1987 and 1994.[4]

But, of course, all is not for the best in the best of all possible worlds. Many researchers in Europe are dissatisfied with measures of absolute poverty like that used in this table. They argue that a poverty standard fixed in absolute terms will lose relevance over time as the general standard of living rises. The poor today are in some senses better off than the richest people who lived in the nineteenth century – even the most deprived now have some access to modern medical treatments, electric light, to television and telephones and all sorts of consumer goods that were simply unavailable a hundred years ago. But that may be little consolation to someone who is at the bottom of the heap and knows it. For this reason, some economists and social scientists believe that measures of *relative* poverty are more meaningful than absolute standards.[5]

Measures of relative poverty ask what proportion of the population is living below a certain percentage of the average standard of living of the population at each point in time. The reference standard of living moves up as the economy becomes more prosperous.

**Table 2**

**Level of Relative Poverty in Ireland, 1994–98**

**Based on a Rising Real-income Standard**

|  | 1994 | 1997 | 1998 |
|---|---|---|---|
| Proportion Falling Below 40% of Standard | 6.8 | 8.1 | 8.8 |
| Proportion Falling Below 50% of Standard | 18.8 | 18.2 | 19.5 |
| Proportion Falling Below 60% of Standard | 29.4 | 30.7 | 29.1 |

Source: *Monitoring Poverty Trends and Exploring Poverty Dynamics in Ireland,* ESRI Policy Research Series 41, June 2001

A mixed picture of the impact of the boom in Irish income distribution emerges from the application of indices of relative poverty. It seems accurate to summarise the evidence as showing that there was no significant trend in the level of relative poverty between 1994–98.[6] (By 'no significant trend' we mean that these measures are all based on sample surveys of about 3,000 households and hence the small variations shown in Table 2 could be due to sampling errors.)

None the less, it is clear that the evidence based on relative income inequality shows a less rosy picture of the effects of the boom than one based on absolute incomes. During the boom, while all income groups enjoyed rising real incomes, those at the bottom of the income distribution tended to fall further behind relative to those at the top. Delving further, we discover that the main reason for this was that those dependent on social welfare payments as their main source of income fell behind in relative terms because these payments, while increasing in real terms, did not increase as fast as after-tax income from employment. This affected the relative position of the elderly in particular, because the standard of living of those dependent on state pensions did not rise as rapidly as those in employment during the mid-1990s. However, since 1998 social welfare pensions have increased by almost one half – the contributory old-age pension rose from €99 in 1998 to €136 in 2001 and €147 in 2002. The 50% increase over the past four years will have significantly improved the relative position of those dependent on these benefits – the group identified as having fared the worst in relative terms over the previous five-year period.

Over the same period the basic-rate child benefit increased from €40 to €118 a month – a threefold increase that will have a dramatic impact on another category affected by poverty – low-income families with dependent children. These developments defuse the criticisms – so often voiced during the boom years – that the incidence of relative poverty increased.

A question to be considered is whether an increase in (relative) inequality is all that detrimental. Economics is about choices and trade-offs. Looking at the broad picture, it seems that countries that place a very strong emphasis on equality pay a price in terms of slower growth. The contrast between the EU and the USA illustrates this. In the EU there is a well-developed welfare state and the income-tax system is progressive, so that the distribution of income tends to be relatively even, at least in principle. The Scandinavian countries come closer to realising this ideal than some other European countries, for example France or Italy. In the US, on the other hand, there is less emphasis on equality, the social welfare system is weaker, and the tax system less progressive. The emphasis is on creating lots of relatively low-income jobs and ensuring that people have the incentive to fill them. The side effect is a very large gap between the rich and the poor.

Falling behind in relative terms means that people become more and more excluded from what is the norm in society. This would

**INCOME TAX AND THE POOR**

In Budget 2002 (December 2001) the Minister proudly proclaimed that the changes in the income-tax code announced in this and the four previous budgets had removed 380,000 lower-paid workers from the tax net. This was because a single person's entry point to income tax was raised from €98 to €209 a week. (Of course, some of these would have come back into the net as their incomes rose.) Yet many commentators claim that recent reductions in tax rates have disproportionately favoured the rich.

In assessing these claims an obvious point is that once a person is out of the income-tax net, his or her situation cannot be made better off by further changes in the tax code. The income-tax system cannot improve the lot of the single people earning less than about €12,000 a year or married couples earning under €24,000. And because average tax rates on incomes just above these thresholds are low, income-tax cuts cannot have a dramatic effect at these income levels. If income tax were abolished on incomes of €40,000 or less, a married couple on €40,000 would be made 12% better off, but a married couple on €30,000 would gain only 6%. This is an inescapable consequence of having a progressive income-tax code.

Having said this, it is possible to target tax changes more accurately at the lower paid by concentrating on increasing the tax-free allowance, widening the standard rate band, and lowering the standard rate as opposed to lowering the higher rate.

Finally, we should not forget that as the burden of income tax on the lower paid has been reduced the proportion of all income receipts raised from the better off has increased. With so many of those on lower incomes now paying little or no income tax, the relatively well off are shouldering an increasing share of the total income-tax bill.

clearly be a problem in the long run but it is less of a concern when the norm is rising as fast as it did in Ireland in the 1990s. With the dizzying growth rates recorded in the 1990s the poor experienced a substantial increase in absolute living standards but still lagged behind the average, and even further behind the substantial crop of 'high flyers' who made their fortunes during the boom. But the poor don't compare themselves with the super-rich; their standards are more modest. A sensible compromise might be to judge the living standards of the poor relative to a norm that is growing by 2%–3% a year. Relative poverty defined in this manner declined in Ireland in the 1990s.

The relevance of this to the Irish experience during the boom is that part of our success in bringing the unemployment rate down from 17% to 4% was due to making the labour market more flexible and giving people incentives to accept job offers, or return to training, rather than remaining unemployed. If this was achieved partly through a rise in the level of relative inequality, many might regard the trade-off as acceptable. Because of the importance of a low unemployment rate in people's feeling of well-being, as shown in a later chapter on quality of life, we authors would be among them. However, we recognise that, if the gap between the 'rich' and 'poor' continues to grow, a point may be reached where social tensions lead to unrest amongst those who feel they have not had their 'fair share' of the success. This may have a damaging effect on society as a whole.

## Preparing for Harder Times

We have emphasised the perhaps unique constellation of positive external factors that supported and sustained the recent growth of the Irish economy. As the 1990s drew to a close several of these drivers of Irish economic growth began to lose momentum.

➢ The bursting of the technology boom on stock markets during 2000 was dramatic. But even more important was the growing awareness that the positive spillover effects of the IT revolution were not as pervasive as had been expected.

➢ The US economic boom turned to recession. This was evident by early in 2001, but after the events of 11 September the downturn gained momentum. The US recession will simultaneously reduce demand for the sectors that have

**THE IMPORTANCE OF OIL PRICES FOR THE GLOBAL ECONOMY**

'Carl Weinberg at High Frequency Economics estimates that the roughly $12 per barrel drop in oil prices from 11 September to 15 November 2001 is equivalent to a $250 billion tax cut for the global economy. That is equivalent to about 1% of global economic activity and dwarfs any fiscal stimulus being discussed by policy makers in world capitals. Christopher André, an economist at the OECD, estimates that a 50% drop in oil prices would add 0.3 percentage points to economic growth in the US and the European Union. Lower oil prices also reduce inflation, allowing interest rates to be lowered.'

Eric Pfanner, 'Plunging Oil Prices: a Shot in the Arm for Ailing World Economies', *International Herald Tribune,* 17 and 18 November 2001

attracted heavy US investment to Ireland and diminish the inflows of projects.

➤ The net contribution of EU aid to the Irish economy had been declining since the early 1990s and this downward trend will accelerate with EU enlargement.

➤ Since the end of 2000 the euro has regained some ground on the foreign exchanges. Many expect that the US dollar will weaken significantly over the medium term. A sharp appreciation of the euro relative to sterling and/or the dollar would expose many sectors to serious difficulties. Such difficulties will be mitigated to the extent that the firms in these sectors have invested in productivity-enhancing technology, information and management systems, developed niche markets that are less sensitive to upward price changes, and acquired productivity enhancing skills in the workforce.

➤ Ireland is very vulnerable to the effects of changes in energy costs. The possibility that the unrest in the Middle East will lead to higher oil prices cannot be ruled out, although the short-run effects of the Afghan conflict were substantially benign from Ireland's point of view. A sharp rise in real oil prices would slow growth. Energy-intensive sectors – including transport and tourism – would be particularly severely hit. The increasingly dispersed settlement pattern that has been a feature of Ireland's housing boom would become even more inappropriate than it is under existing conditions.

➢ A low corporation tax (CT) rate has been among Ireland's most important attractions as a location for foreign investment. Our success in attracting FDI in the financial and 'high tech' sectors inevitably provoked complaints of 'unfair tax competition' from other EU member states. Pressures for tax harmonisation across EU countries drew attention to Ireland's low tax rate as a possible distortion of the common market. The new uniform corporation tax rate of 12.5% will apply from 2003. This will entail a significant increase in the tax liabilities of companies at present paying at the 10% rate, while at the same time major European countries like Germany have reduced their corporation tax rates. And it is striking that part of the stimulus package announced by President George Bush in the wake of the events of 11 September 2001 is a reduction in the burden of corporate tax in the US in order to encourage US firms to invest at home rather than abroad. The Irish advantage on the corporation tax front is being eroded and this trend will continue.

While firms may be attracted to and anchored in locations by agglomeration economies – that is, the advantages of operating in an area where a concentration of similar firms has created deep labour, capital and sub-supply markets – they are increasingly sensitive to tax differentials. A recent study concluded that 'taxes appear to be an important consideration for firms' decisions whether or not to invest abroad, as well as where to invest abroad.'[7]

Because a low corporation tax rate has been a significant factor in attracting FDI to Ireland, it is important to consider the possible effect of a narrowing of tax differentials on these flows. It has been estimated that the increase in the Irish statutory CT rate from 10% to

12.5% will reduce the inflow of FDI to the country by about 7%.[8] But the effects of this would be minor compared with those of a more thorough harmonisation of EU CT rates. It has been estimated that if CT rates had been harmonised on the EU average over the period 1990-1997 Ireland would have experienced a fall of more than 1.3% of GDP per annum in its net FDI flows.[9] There would also have been a fall of about 0.8% of GDP in revenue from this tax. It is therefore clear that the attractiveness of Ireland's low CT regime to inward FDI is vulnerable to the growing concerns about unfair tax competition and the pressure towards more harmonised EU tax rates.

In Ireland the era of falling taxes came to an end in 2001. To the extent that falling taxes spurred economic growth, it is reasonable to conclude that this source of stimulus is now gone. There are, however, favourable factors that will help Ireland ride out the current period.

The public finances are in good shape. Although the buoyancy of tax revenue on which we had come to depend for so long disappeared in the course of 2001, and current spending is rising very rapidly, there is no need to contemplate the sort of drastic cutbacks in capital spending that occurred in the late 1980s. While the need to curb the spiral of current spending has become more urgent, the level of spending on badly needed infrastructure improvements should be maintained. It would be a departure from previous recessions if fiscal policy were counter-cyclical – that is, if the contribution of public spending and taxation helped offset rather than aggravated the recessionary trend of other components of aggregate demand. Not that all other components of spending are likely to collapse. Disposable incomes have risen rapidly due to reductions in the burden of taxation and large pay increases, and, combined with low interest rates, this will help maintain consumer expenditure.

## Lessons for the Future

We have seen that much of what has given us our boom – significant transfers from the EU, a soft exchange rate relative to our main trading partners, the sustained US economic boom, the impact of IT on productivity, and low energy prices – is outside our control. Of these elements, the first three are no longer working for us. The IT productivity contribution, to the extent that it exists at all, is likely to be a diminishing influence in the future. There is an ever-present danger that oil prices will move sharply upward, associated with disruption in the Gulf states.

If all of these previously benign external factors were to move against us, our adaptive abilities would be tested to the limit. But the economy will suffer less during the current slowdown the more we can reinforce our remaining strengths. Three principles should inform our reaction. The first is maximising the efficiency with which we spend public money. One of the great positive differences between now and the eighties is that the public-sector balance sheet is healthy. The level of debt has declined dramatically relative to GDP. Another positive factor is that, in order to qualify for European Union funds, we have had to develop integrated economic development strategies that are, in the main, coherent and mutually reinforcing. But this advantage can very easily be undermined if we are not vigilant, if we maintain the volume of the investment programme but choose the wrong mix of projects and programmes, and if the public are not well informed as to what is being done on their behalf and why. By 'efficiency' we mean ensuring that the objectives we have agreed as regards both public investment and current expenditure in education, social services, health, transport, farming, tourism, energy etc. are met with the minimum possible expenditure, i.e., that we as tax payers get as much as possible out of the money that is spent on our behalf. This requires that serious and substantive analysis of the benefits and costs of alternatives be undertaken, that maximum use be made of competitive tendering, and information be available to all via web sites and otherwise as to the decisions being taken and their rationale. If we maintain the public investment programmes as laid out in our National Plan 2001–2006, and ensure that this money is spent well, our credibility

## THE USE OF REGULATORY IMPACT ASSESSMENT BY THE US ENVIRONMENT PROTECTION AGENCY

'Under Executive Order 12291 of 1981, the US Environment Protection Agency is required to analyse major regulatory proposals with a view to identifying the alternative which maximises the "net benefits to society". The contents of each Regulatory Impact Assessment (RIA) must include a description of the potential net benefits of the rule, a description of the potential costs, and an identification of those likely to bear the costs a determination of the potential net benefits, a description of alternative approaches that could substantially achieve the same goal at lower costs. In an examination of three of the regulations proposed over the 1981–1986 period – lead in fuels, used oil, and pre-manufacture review – it was estimated that net benefits of over $10 billion were gained by changes made in the proposed regulations as a result of the analyses.'

US Office of Policy Analysis, 1987

will be enhanced, the downward draught from external negative forces will be mitigated, and we will ensure that we have a strong platform from which to take advantage of the upturn when it comes.

The second principle is fairness, the attempt to ensure that the burden of adjustment to adversity is distributed fairly across our community. This is perhaps the most difficult challenge – as Albert Camus observed, 'We are all special cases.' But the most vulnerable are not difficult to identify, and should be protected from the worst ravages of adjustment.

The third principle is flexibility and adaptability, the willingness to innovate. Among the factors under our control that contributed to the boom of the 1990s we listed the elastic supply of good-quality and relatively inexpensive labour, our flexible labour-market practices, and the industrial peace that prevailed. As the other drivers of the boom weaken, we have to place greater reliance on these strengths. The true test of how thoroughly the economy was transformed during the 1990s will be the contribution of labour-market flexibility to the adjustments required by our changing economic situation.

## EDUCATION AND THE URBAN INSTITUTE OF IRELAND

Education, education, education, the three most important attributes in helping individuals and their country fulfil their potential. We in Ireland have been investing heavily in first, second and tertiary levels, and this has been crucial in sustaining our economic and social progress.

The next stage in this progression is investment in research and development, in the creation and application of new knowledge, and the fostering of innovation. The Higher Education Authority (HEA) is the government agency charged with leading the innovation wave at the universities. One strand of this programme is the creation of interdisciplinary and inter-institutional centres of research excellence. The Urban Institute of Ireland is a product of this initiative. It is a powerhouse for developing new ideas designed to improve the quality of the urban working and living environment.

Created under the leadership of University College Dublin in partnership with Trinity College, and with the collaboration of other institutions, it is the only centre of its kind in Ireland and is unique also in a European context. More than seventy researchers in architecture, economics, civil/mechanical/structural engineering, environmental studies, geography, planning, sociology and archaeology are already involved in carrying out Urban Institute-sponsored projects. The authors of this book have been involved in the development of this concept, and its implementation.

Specifically, the adjustment will be aided by the willingness of those in employment to accept flexibility in regard to pay and working conditions and by the willingness of those unfortunate enough to lose their jobs to move to new locations and occupations, to retrain, and to accept new employment offers on less favourable terms. The short-term pain involved will minimise the longer-term pain as the economy returns to full employment in the longer run.

# CHAPTER 3

# The Importance of Productivity

'How many Irishmen does it take to screw in a lightbulb?' The fading image of Feckless Paddy has seen a commensurate fading of the Irish joke. And it all has to do with productivity, the output per person in the economy. In this chapter we look at this issue, which is central to understanding past growth and the prospects for sustainable improvements in living standards in the future.

## Productivity

Economic growth implies that the economy is getting bigger – more is being produced, national income is rising and so on. But living standards are what really matter, not the size of the economy. A larger economy does not necessarily imply commensurate increases in income per person. For this reason the distinction between the growth of *total* output and output *per capita* is crucial. The economy must grow faster than the population if there is to be any improvement in living standards. Now, in the long run the labour force will tend to increase at the same rate as the population (when participation rates are stable), so improvements in living standards depend on the growth of productivity, that is, output per person employed or indeed per hour worked.[1] We believe that too much discussion of the performance of the Irish economy concentrated on the growth of GDP rather than of GDP *per capita* or output per

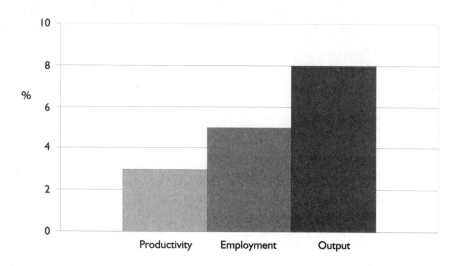

Figure 5: OUTPUT AND PRODUCTIVITY GROWTH, 1993–2000,
ANNUAL AVERAGE GROWTH RATES

person employed, so in this chapter we focus on the growth of productivity during the period of the Celtic Tiger.

## Growth – Intensive and Extensive

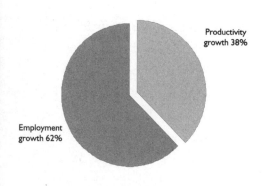

Figure 6: CONTRIBUTIONS OF EMPLOYMENT AND
PRODUCTIVITY TO GROWTH

We focus on an issue that we regard as fundamental from a policy perspective, namely the contributions of the growth of employment and of productivity growth to total growth during the Irish boom. As we stated above, in the long run improvement in living standards depends on the growth of output per person employed rather than the growth of total output. More generally, the key to economic success in the long run is the more efficient use of available resources, especially labour, rather than the employment of additional resources at the same level of efficiency. We call the component of growth due to rising productivity 'intensive growth' and that due to the use of more inputs, especially labour, 'extensive growth'.

Figure 5 decomposes Ireland's growth since 1993 into these constituents. Between 1993 and 2000 real GNP grew by 8% and employment grew by 5% a year, so output per person employed grew by 3% a year.[2] Thus over 60% of the growth in output was due to the growth in employment or extensive growth (Figure 6). While the 3% annual growth in output per worker is a very respectable achievement by international standards, it is much less 'miraculous' that the more widely cited growth in total output. It is also striking that estimates of the contribution of productivity to the growth of the economy over the long run shows only a slight upturn in the 1990s. There was no marked surge in productivity growth during the recent boom.

It is instructive to further decompose the 5% annual growth in the numbers at work into the part due to the growth of the population of working age and that due to the rise in the employment/population ratio. Between 1993 and 2000 the population aged 15 and over increased at an annual average rate of 1.6%. While this was exceptionally high by European standards, it accounted for only about one-third of the total growth in employment – the remainder came from the rise in the employment/population ratio from 44.5% in 1993 to 56.4% in 2000. Moreover, we must bear in mind that our measure of productivity is over-generous because it does not adjust for the distorting effect of MNCs on our conventional measures of output.

The two charts can be combined into a chart that illustrates the relative contribution of (i) productivity growth, (ii) the growth of

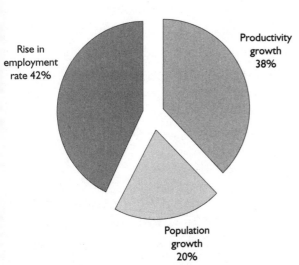

Rise in employment rate 42%

Productivity growth 38%

Population growth 20%

Figure 7: SOURCES OF GROWTH 1993–2001

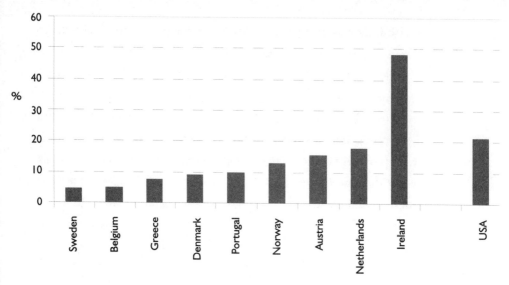

Figure 8: INCREASE IN NUMBERS AT WORK, 1993–2000

the population of working age, and (iii) the rising employment rate, to the economic boom of the 1990s (Figure 7). Increased productivity accounted for less than 40% of the total growth of output, population growth for 20%, and the remaining 40% was due to the rise in the employment rate.

The rate of growth of employment in Ireland during the 1990s was exceptional by European standards, as is illustrated by Figure 8, which compares the percentage increase in employment since 1993 in seven smaller European countries and the USA. The percentage increase in employment in Ireland was almost 2.7 times that of the next best-performing economy, the Netherlands, and four to five times those of Sweden, Norway, Denmark and Belgium.[3] The Irish record was also far more impressive than the much-praised US 'jobs machine'.

The rapid growth of employment has been the really exceptional feature of Ireland's recent boom. The boom in employment has been particularly welcome in a country where for decades the total number at work stagnated and the natural growth of the population was siphoned off through emigration or, when that safety valve was closed by the global recession of the 1980s, rising unemployment.

Ireland's exceptional rate of employment growth was facilitated by a very elastic supply of labour.[4] The elastic labour supply allowed employment to grow at an exceptional pace without – until 1999-2000 – reaching the point at which labour shortages led to significant wage inflation. This combination was facilitated by the contribution of the partnership process to wage moderation.

The factors that accounted for the highly elastic labour supply therefore lie at the heart of the Irish economic 'miracle'. They include the following:

> The large initial pool of unemployment. The unemployment rate fell from 15.7% in 1993 to under 4% by the end of 2000, and this alone accounted for over 100,000 additional workers.

> The working-age population grew very rapidly as the baby boom of the 1960s and 1970s came on the labour market. As the economic boom gathered pace, these young people were absorbed into employment in Ireland rather than having to emigrate, as had been the norm for a majority even as recently as the 1980s.

> Once the boom got underway the openness of the labour market led to a sizeable net inflow of population. In recent years immigration has accounted for about half of the growth of the labour force.

> Women's labour-force participation rates had been rising slowly, but the rate of increase accelerated sharply during the economic boom.

Falling unemployment, rising labour-force participation rates, and the changing age structure of the population all contributed to the rising employment/population ratio. Without any improvement in productivity or increase in the working-age population, the higher employment rate accounted for 40% of the growth of output that was recorded since 1993. But a rising employment/population ratio is a transitional phenomenon. The Irish rate has already reached the

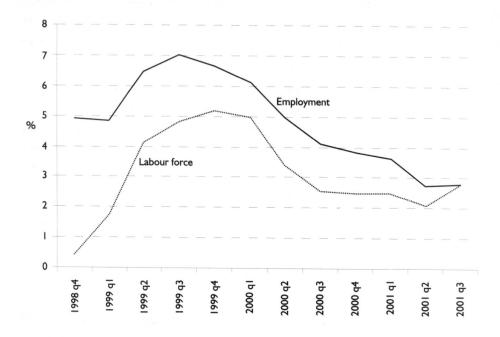

Figure 9: GROWTH OF EMPLOYMENT AND THE LABOUR FORCE

European average and the contribution of further increases to future employment growth will fall from now on. Furthermore, the 'natural growth' of the working-age population is also slowing down. The numbers leaving the educational system peaked in 1999-2000. That leaves net immigration as the remaining potential source of labour-force increase. We discuss the policy issues raised by reliance on immigration below, but we consider it unlikely that this source will augment the labour force by much more than 0.5% a year.

In fact, the growth of the labour force has been falling since 1999 (Figure 9). It peaked at an amazing 5% in the late 1990s, falling back to just half that rate by 2001, while growth in the numbers at work has fallen from over 7% to 3.6%. These short-term indicators are straws in the wind. Recent population and labour-force projections suggest that even if a generous allowance is made for continued increases in labour-force participation rates and substantial net immigration, the rate of increase of the labour force will decline to an annual average rate of 1.7% (or about 30,000 a year) over the period 2001–2006. While still high by international standards, this is much lower than the exceptional rate recorded in recent years.

If a 3% rate of growth of output per person at work can be maintained and the rate of growth of the labour force falls to about 1.5%, the long-term sustainable growth rate of the economy is 4.5%. While very high by international standards, this might seem like a recession by comparison with the growth recorded in the 1990s.

Slower growth of the labour force implies slower growth of total output, but there is a world of difference between a three-percentage-points fall in the output growth rate due to a corresponding fall in the labour force and one that is due entirely to a fall in the growth of output per worker or a rise in unemployment.

The issue of 'how fast can an economy grow' has been hotly debated in the United States in recent years. The question posed is whether the rise in the US growth rate in the second half of the 1990s reflects factors that will be sustainable in the longer run (such as a rise

## SETTING THE SPEED LIMIT

Two prominent economists reflect our own view on the limits of IT as a contributor to economic growth.

'The "new economy" view is that the impact of IT is like phlogiston, an invisible substance that spills over into every kind of economic activity and reveals its presence by increases in industry-level productivity growth across the US economy. This view is simply inconsistent with the empirical evidence.

'Our results suggest that ... productivity growth in the production of IT is responsible for a sizeable part of the recent spurt in Total Factor Productivity growth ... However, there has been no corresponding eruption of industry-level productivity growth in these sectors that would herald the arrival of phlogiston-like spillovers from production in the IT sectors.'

Dale W. Jorgenson and Kevin J. Stiroh, 'Raising the Speed Limit: U.S. Economic Growth in the Information Age', *Brookings Papers on Economic Activity* 2000:1, pp. 125–236 in productivity due, for example, to the impact of new information technologies on the economy), or whether it was due to transitory factors, such as falling unemployment and rising labour-force participation rates. Economists have been generally sceptical of building a higher growth rate into the projections on which long-run fiscal trends are based. The majority feel that the evidence does not support the view that there has been a major shift in the trend rate of productivity growth that will propel the US economy to significantly higher growth rates in the medium term. The consensus is that the growth of the US economy will average about 3.5% a year in the first decade of this century. The labour force (hours worked) will grow by about 1.75%, so output per worker is expected to grow by about 2% to 2.5%. These projections highlight the exceptional performance of the Irish economy over the 1990s.

A point to bear in mind is that forecasts of the average growth rate in the long term are likely to be more accurate than attempts to predict short-term turning points. During the year 2001 we had a dramatic illustration of the uncertainty of short-term predictions. No one foresaw how rapidly the growth rate would fall and forecasts made at the start of the year were revised sharply downwards as the year progressed.

## Lessons for the Future

The message of this chapter has been about the importance of productivity growth as a determinant of the trend in living standards. It makes a lot of difference whether productivity grows at 1.5% or 3% a year. At the lower growth rate it takes 46 years for living standards to double, at the higher only 23 years. A country that lags behind in productivity growth will inevitably experience a fall in its relative standard of living.

The forces that drive productivity growth are widely recognised. The ideal combination is a well-educated and adaptable labour force working with new technologies and up-to-date physical capital (such as machinery and buildings). Foreign direct investment can be a powerful vector of transmission of new technologies embodied in new capital. The virtuous circle in which FDI is attracted by an adaptable and educated labour force and then raises its productivity was an important part of the story of Ireland's success in the 1990s. We must continue to foster these conditions, so that the pace of productivity growth does not falter. At the same time it is also vital to foster more indigenous innovation and enterprise, as indeed has been a declared goal of Irish industrial policy over the years.

The lesson to be drawn is the urgency of maintaining the emphasis on productivity-enhancing investments in both human and physical capital. Henry Ford observed: 'If you don't buy a machine you need, you pay for it without getting it.' This issue of capturing productivity gain is as important today as it was a century and a half ago. As the extensive component of our growth tapers off, the need to achieve the maximum possible rate of productivity growth becomes increasingly urgent. This means maintaining our investment in education, so that we have the embedded skills that allow productivity to continue. There is no room for the complacency that tends to creep in when reviewing the contribution of education to the miracle years of the 1990s. True, the rising educational standards of the workforce accounted for a significant proportion of the growth of output during the boom as participation in secondary and tertiary education rose to European levels. But there is room for further increases in participation and, more importantly, for improvements in the numeracy and literacy standards attained at each level of the system. Although different indicators reveal different pictures, there is plenty of room for raising standards and outcomes. Moreover, although a substantial increase in scientific research in now occurring, we still have to meet the challenge of establishing in Ireland significant centres of world-class applied technological research and university–industry interaction of the type that has made Massachusetts and California, for example, magnets for the highest levels of industrial research and development.

Finally, returning to the growth pause that is now underway, even if emigration from Ireland were temporarily to become a feature of our economy again, those of us who go abroad do so with skills that allow us to both fulfil and develop our potential, so that if we return to Ireland we have much to offer. It is likely that our recent growth has been sustained for so long in part because of the reservoir of talented and skilled Irish people who went abroad in the eighties, then came back a decade later and gave us all the benefit of their enhanced capacities. And our willingness to move out and then back has benefited us as individuals and as a society, as has the emphasis since the 1960s on the importance of attracting inward investment in technologically advanced sectors. Openness to new ideas and new ways of doing things will remain essential if a high rate of productivity growth is to be maintained. A key to attracting talent is the availability of affordable housing, ease of getting to and from work, and a high quality of life generally. We address these issues later on.

# CHAPTER 4

# Globalisation:
# The Faustian Bargain

There is now some popular disenchantment with ideas that only a short time ago seemed to command widespread support and respect. Globalisation or 'international economic integration' is one such.

'If you want attention, start a fight.' Seattle, Prague, Gothenburg, Nice, Genoa, cities once renowned for their architecture or civic-mindedness, are now a litany to disillusion with, and antagonism to, globalism in general, and unfettered free trade in particular. They also epitomise the speed and power of media images. One brick thrown through one window in McDonald's on Vasagaten in Gothenburg is seen by over five hundred million people thirty minutes after the event. Many see global trade as the unaccountable and ungainly bull in the national china shop – uncontrollable destruction randomly dispensed, with the poorest least able to protect themselves. And a sense of vulnerability finds expression in disillusion with politics and the political process.

To add to the confusion there is no agreed definition of 'globalisation'. The protestors are happy to use intercontinental air travel, the Internet, mobile phones and faxes to organise their confrontations, ignoring the irony that these are ingredients of the globalisation that so infuriates them. The spread of English as a global language helps them as much as it helps their *bêtes noires*. Maybe MacDonald's – that prime target of protestors' anger – would have been well advised to have adopted a different logo in each country – as General Motors uses brand names like Opel and Vauxhall to retain German and British loyalty to old national marques. But in reality the protests have been more about symbols and style than about substance. A lack of clarity over what exactly is being opposed never detracts from a good protest or revolution.

Let us look at the background to this unrest. The world economy became increasingly integrated in the course of the nineteenth century due to the dramatic fall in the cost of communications and transport and because of liberal economic policies. This globalisation played a large part in the unprecedented expansion of population and wealth recorded over the century. Mass emigration from Ireland was part of the phenomenon, and, painful though it was, it helped raise the living standards of those who stayed behind as well as those who left. There was more land and livestock to go around among fewer farmers. The effects of economic integration were also visible in the way food and commodity prices moved closer together around the world – the price of grain and corn in the US mid-west affected the price of pigs at fairs in the west of Ireland. The discipline of the market place forced a reallocation of resources to their most efficient uses. While this entailed wrenching dislocation for many, the increase in wealth it generated led in the long run to an improvement in living standards for most.

The First World War and the currency instability of the inter-war period checked the growing integration of the world economy. But even in the 1920s the world economy retained the most important features of Victorian international capitalism. The deathblow came with the Great Depression. The Wall Street collapse and the ensuing breakdown of the US economy rapidly spread to Europe, Latin America and other regions of the world. The flip side of the benefits of integration was suddenly apparent. It became almost impossible to defend the case for globalisation. In 1920 John Maynard Keynes had enthused about the creative power of liberal capitalism that allowed him to trade exotic commodities on world markets by telephone while sipping his morning tea in bed, while British venture capital was transforming cities from Buenos Aires to Shanghai. But thirteen years later in a famous address in University College Dublin – attended by members of the newly elected protectionist Fianna Fáil government as well as of the outgoing Cumann na nGaedheal party – he endorsed the homespun economic policies of the new government and acknowledged that the Victorian economic order had failed, for the time being at least.

The retreat to isolationism triggered by the Great Depression resulted in a collapse of globalisation so severe that by some measures the level of economic integration reached in the 1920s was not regained until the 1970s.

So, one lesson of history is that recessions are bad for globalisation. An economy that is closely integrated into the global economy cannot insulate itself when the rest of the world goes into recession and international trade spirals downwards. On such occasions the wider public – and not just the crew that roams the world protesting against globalisation even in good times – becomes worried about the lack of national control over economic policy. The risk of a backlash and a retreat into isolationism grows.

Few countries were as thorough in their rejection of globalisation as Ireland was between the 1930s and the 1960s. Our system of industrial protectionism was radical and far-reaching. We tried to live up to Jonathan Swift's advice to burn everything British but their coal. Our domestic consumer market was effectively isolated from imports, even though we remained dependent on imported raw materials and capital equipment. International flows of money were minimised, especially after the war, by an elaborate system of exchange controls. Only our labour market remained integrated into the wider market beyond our shores, and during the Second World War the availability of employment in Britain attracted massive numbers of Irish men and women whose aspirations could not be met in the stagnant Irish economy. When the Irish economy experienced yet more setbacks during the 1950s the emigrants flowed out on a scale that had not been experienced since the desperate 1880s, but now they were more likely to go to British cities and building sites rather than across the Atlantic Ocean. This period brought home to Irish policy makers the failure of economic policies that had been carried forward from the 1930s far beyond their 'sell by' date.

The gathering momentum of the move towards European economic integration and the prospect of British entry to the European Economic Community (EEC) made it inevitable that Ireland would have to open up to the wider world once again. The key event was the signing of the Anglo-Irish Free Trade Area Agreement in 1965, which prepared the path for entry into the EEC in 1973. The isolation of the previous forty years was being buried. Its final death knell was sounded by the ratification of the Single European Act (1987) and the Maastricht Treaty (1992). The fixing of the value of the Irish pound to the common European currency, the euro, in 1999 was the last and most dramatic move on the path to Ireland's full reintegration into the European and wider world economy.

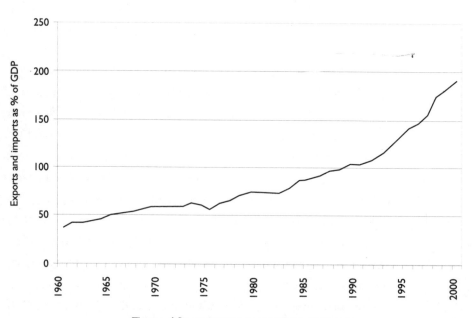

Figure 10: OPENNESS OF THE IRISH ECONOMY

The ratio of exports to national product (GDP) is a convenient measure of the openness of an economy. Figure 10 shows how much more open the Irish economy became after 1960 and especially as the boom of the 1990s gathered momentum.[1]

This opening up of the economy was not the outcome of a careful strategy or conviction in the merits of free trade. In fact, the 1958 government document *Economic Development* that is usually credited with charting the way out of the doldrums of the 1950s was quite cautious on the question, pointing out that 'should Ireland become a member of the proposed European Free Trade Area she should be dispensed from undertaking the full obligations of membership until her economy has attained a satisfactory relationship with those of the more highly industrialised members.' It still saw agriculture as the locomotive of Irish economic development and had no vision of the boom, based on industrial exports, that was eventually to transform the economy in the 1990s.

Even if Ireland's move from import substitution to export promotion was driven by the failure of the former rather than a strong belief in the latter, the result of this shift was dramatic. A comparison of the growth of the economy in the years 1950 to 1960 with that over the following fifteen years shows how much the performance of the economy improved after the opening up to the rest of the world. Of course, openness did not protect us from the policy mistakes of the late 1970s, and the 'hangover' of the 1980s was severe and long-lasting. But the combination of sound domestic policies and a booming world economy finally paid off handsomely in the 1990s, when the Irish economy surpassed all its historical and most international benchmarks. We may well look back on the 1990s as a golden age, a period when openness to inflows of foreign capital and markets led to an unprecedented and subsequently unsurpassed growth of living standards and employment. This was when we were at last admitted to the catch-up game and virtually eliminated the gap in living standards with the rich countries of the world.

The transition from an inward-looking economy, dependent on

**IRELAND HEADS WORLD INDEX OF GLOBALISATION**

That was a headline in the *Financial Times* (9 January 2002). It was based on a study of trends in economic integration, international political engagement, personal contacts and the take-up of information technology, which found that Ireland is by far the world's most globalised country, way ahead of countries like Japan, the US, the UK, or even Singapore. We score high not only on the importance of trade, financial inflows, and foreign direct investment, but also on the level of global personal contacts. Interestingly, the study also found a link between globalisation and prosperity and concluded that people who are happy with life tend to be globally integrated!

jobs in subsistence agriculture and inefficient, protected industries, to our present outward-looking economy, with its exceptional openness to international trade and dependence on inward investment in high-tech but mostly foreign-owned industries, was facilitated by the growth of new, better-paid employment opportunities that more than offset the loss of jobs in the protected sectors. Large inflows of EU aid, especially agricultural subsidies, also helped.

To the historian it seems obvious that Ireland's success has been based on the opening up of the economy, but with the passage of time and as memories of the bad old days of isolationism faded it was to be expected that enthusiasm for international integration would decline. This may be roughly charted in the voting behaviour of the electorate on EU referenda. In 1972, 71% of the voters turned out to vote on our accession to the EEC and of these 83% voted 'yes' – this means that 59% of those eligible to vote approved our entry to the EEC. In June 2001 a mere 35% of the voters turned out for the referendum on the Treaty of Nice and of those only 46% voted 'yes' – the proportion of eligible voters voting 'yes' fell to 16%. Although many other issues were involved, this drop in support for an EU initiative is surely an indication of flagging enthusiasm among Irish voters for the particular form that globalisation is taking in Europe. The only clear message that can be taken from the incoherent campaign and vote on the Nice

Treaty is that 'anti-globalisation' is on the rise in Ireland.

To what, then, should we attribute the growth of anti-globalisation sentiment in Ireland? The answer to this lies in the nature of the Faustian bargain that is globalisation.

Economists recognise the impossibility of reconciling the following desiderata:

> Free trade

> Fixed exchange rates or the use of a common currency

> Free movement of capital into and out of the country

> An acceptable degree of national economic autonomy.

Each has considerable advantages, but all four cannot be combined. Membership of the EU has allowed Ireland to achieve virtually complete free trade and free movement of capital, as well as the stability afforded by the use of the euro, even if our situation in this regard is somewhat compromised by the UK's absence from the euro club. But this has all come at a price in terms of domestic economic autonomy.

Consider the constraints that have been placed on our policy makers:

> The adoption of the euro has removed exchange-rate and monetary policy from Dublin's Dame Street to Frankfurt's Kaiserallee.

> Our fiscal policy is constrained by the Stability Pact – the threat that if we returned to the bad habits of the late 1970s we would be subject to large fines payable to Frankfurt. Even though we were nowhere near violating the terms of the pact, Minister for Finance Charlie McCreevy was treated to an unprecedented rebuke from Commissioner Pedro Solbes in spring 2001 because his budget was deemed to be too exuberant by experts in Brussels. Many EU member states are bumping up against this constraint as the global economy moves into recession; their freedom to implement counter-cyclical fiscal policies is

constrained by a pact that was never formally approved by their electorates.

➤ Industrial promotion by our development agencies is tightly constrained by the Treaty of Rome and other EU legislation. Narrow limits are placed on the aid that can be offered to domestic or overseas firms to persuade them to locate in Ireland. Aid to distressed sectors and companies has to be approved by Brussels.

➤ Regional policy is similarly constrained. Even the definition of disadvantaged regions has been vetted and changed by European experts. The level of regional aids is limited to relatively small variations on the permissible level of general industrial aids.

➤ A low rate of corporation tax has been the mainstay of Irish industrial policy since the 1960s. It is one of the more enlightened economic-policy initiatives we undertook as an independent state. But Europe can be critical of good as well as of bad national policies and our low tax rate has been attacked by Europe. Even raising the tax rate to 12.5% and extending it uniformly to all sectors may not insulate us from further pressure to 'harmonise' on the higher average rate prevailing in the EU.

The last point is particularly salient. Amid the economic policies pursued since independence, the use of a low tax rate on industry to attract export-oriented inward investment to Ireland stands out as both sensible and successful. To have it questioned or censured by the EU is a sensitive example of the constraints imposed by globalisation on national economic policies that deserve general support.

A transfer of power to remote institutions insulated from national politics is an essential ingredient of membership of the EU. The European Central Bank is designed to be as aloof as possible from the pressures of national politics. It has to worry only about inflation. The *contretemps* between Ireland's Minister for Finance and the European Commissioner over the appropriateness of Budget 2001 was a far more rigorous examination than any minister has ever undergone in set-piece post-budget debates in Dáil Éireann. The debate between Upper Merrion Street (Department of Finance) and the experts in Brussels about Ireland's corporate tax structures has also been far more intense and sophisticated than any that took place in Ireland.

Many economists would immediately point out that these constraints are broadly beneficial. Freedom to devalue the currency, to push down interest rates and incur large fiscal deficits, is not the road to prosperity. Some economists question the wisdom of any grants or subsidies to industry when it is hard to avoid significant waste and deadweight in this area. Irish economists are not alone in tending to distrust their politicians in the sphere of economic policy. In fact, elegant papers have been written to show that the more remote from the voters the policy makers are, the better the economic outcome in the long run.

It is also possible to point to the massive improvements that the EU has made in many aspects of Irish policy making. Irish planning for capital spending has become much more sophisticated under the discipline of applying for EU aid. Our reluctant deregulation of several sectors of the economy – telecommunications and energy, for example – has been forced on us by an impatient EU Commission and it is also likely that much of our privatisation of state-owned enterprises would not have come about without persistent prodding from Europe. And if we had been waiting for domestic policy makers to tackle our numerous environmental problems – water and air quality, waste disposal, sewage improvements, etc – we would be waiting still for even the modest improvements that have been achieved. (Of course, at the same time the EU should be castigated for many idiotic policies they have forced on member states in this area, especially for the damage done to the environment by the Common Agricultural Policy as well as some of the perversities of the fisheries policy, but that's another story.) Finally, European competition policy has introduced rigour in an area that Irish policy makers never took seriously.

It is also easy to exaggerate the degree to which globalisation, even membership of the EU, has eroded national economic sovereignty. True, the Irish economy is very small – amounting to a mere 1% of the total EU. And by comparison with the larger multinational companies, the Irish state may appear puny. But despite claims from some quarters to the contrary, multinational corporations do not seriously threaten the powers of the nation state. This threat is often measured by comparing the turnover of large corporations with the value added (GDP) of a small country, but the comparison is spurious. Microsoft is one of the world's largest corporations but its value added is a mere $20 billion compared to Ireland's GDP of $100 billion. In addition, no corporation, no matter how large, has the power, much less the right, to raise taxes, conduct foreign policy, conscript an army or imprison people, but even the smallest national government can legally do all these things. True, internationally mobile capital tends to seek out locations that are favourable (i.e. profitable) and exert a degree of influence on national policies. And multinational corporations can be ruthless in their pursuit of profits – their shareholders are an impatient lot. But they remain subject to national and international law, and have been frequently brought to book for anti-competitive practices, environmental damage and so on. And they cannot rival the power that governments derive from their power to raise taxes. The governments of the EU member states control on average about 40% of their national economies by raising and spending tax revenue. Moreover, there are still significant differences in the role of the state between countries even within the EU – at one extreme lies Sweden, where the state raises about 57% in taxes, at the other lies Ireland where the state raises 'only' 33% of GDP in taxes, so that economic integration has not forced nations to adopt a single model for the role of the state or placed a straitjacket on social and economic policy.[2]

But this is not the point. The point is that national policy makers are becoming more impotent in the economic sphere and this is becoming increasingly clear to the electorate. In good times this is not a problem. When a booming world economy spills over into Ireland and grants and aids flow abundantly from the EU there is ample compensation for the loss of national economic sovereignty. But as economic growth slows and the funds from Brussels taper off, the electorate wants its elected national politicians to 'do something'. The gloss wears off globalisation when elected politicians have to say, 'We can't because we are bound by this or that treaty.'

In other parts of the world the process of transferring power from the nation state and its politicians to international institutions has gone even further. In as many as forty or fifty countries around the world – most of them poor and crisis-ridden – the power of economic policy making has been transferred to economists at the International Monetary Fund (IMF) and the World Bank in Washington, DC. Joseph Stiglitz, one of the 2001 winners of the Nobel Prize in economics, is strongly critical of the 'Washington consensus' that underpins the policies imposed by these institutions on poor countries. (Of course, the US government is under no pressure to follow such advice.) Indeed he resigned his position as Chief Economist at the World Bank because of his belief that a free-market economic model was being uncritically applied in situations around the world where the preconditions for its successful operation simply do not exist. No wonder these 'Bretton Woods' institutions are clearly in the sights of the anti-globalisation protestors. The phenomenon we are describing has been labelled the 'Argentinisation' of economic policy because that country prior to January 2002 was a prime example of one that had virtually handed over all economic policy making to outside agencies; the Argentinian currency board made the Federal Reserve (the US Central Bank) the real Central Bank of Argentina, and the need to reassure international financial markets obliged the government to comply with a long list of conditions from the IMF. Meanwhile, interest rates have soared, the economy stagnated and political and social unrest mounts. Despite signing up to many good policies, the country is entering its fourth year of profound recession.

The Irish economy is in a much stronger situation than Argentina's, of course. We have clearly gained enormously through the move from protectionism to free trade. The deregulation of the

**FAIR TRADE**

'During the original Uruguay Round [1986], which led to the creation of the World Trade Organisation, rich countries pledged to open their markets to textiles, crops and other basic exports from the developing world. There has been some progress in that area, but arcane customs rules, unnecessary red tape, stingy quotas and anti-dumping programs still keep poor nations' exports out of wealthy markets.'

Editorial, *International Herald Tribune*, 10–11 November 2001, p.8

economy – although far from complete – has, on balance, been very beneficial. So we have every reason to hope that we will continue to prosper as we become more closely integrated into the world economic system. But the recent fall in the growth rate is partly a side-effect of the extreme openness of our economy and the current synchronisation of the global business cycle. Moreover, our EU commitments have made national politicians increasingly less able to influence, or even to appear to influence, key areas of the economy. When analysed with dispassionate economic logic this may be all to the good, but it does illustrate the democratic deficit that is an intrinsic part of the globalisation bargain we have made. As long as strong economic growth delivers visible benefits the electorate may well be happy to pay this price. But if the chill winds of world recession deprive us of these benefits, albeit only temporarily, it is hard to predict where the political forces that ultimately dictate which economic system we wish to adopt will lead us.

It is sobering to bear in mind that the Nice Treaty was rejected by the Irish electorate *before* there was much concrete evidence that the global slow-down spreading from the US was going to do serious damage to the Irish economy. In the first half of 2001 we were more concerned about the impact of foot and mouth disease than with the adverse effect of the technology bust in the US, let alone the aftermath of the events of 11 September. It was also before the EU vetoed further state aid to the state airline, Aer Lingus. These issues might have made voters even more sceptical of the benefits of globalisation.

But the mood swings of public opinion are unpredictable. The outrages of 11 September 2001 have left the protestors in some disarray, while it has made 'the establishment' more aware of the terrible risks inherent in globalisation. Let us hope that a balanced assessment will emerge from the cross-currents of this debate.

## Lessons for the Future

For Ireland, it is important to maintain the degree of openness to world markets that we have already achieved. The dark days of the 1950s, when we sat in self-imposed purdah, shielded from the world, its markets and even its ideas, and reaped the whirlwind of poverty, unemployment and mass emigration, must never be repeated. But we need also to be sensitive to the fact that global free trade as it has evolved and as we have participated in it is not equally beneficial to all. Specifically, many less developed countries that are in the agriculture and natural resource-dependent phase of their development still find that the global system discriminates against their interest. The European Union prohibits or limits imports of agricultural product not produced within the Union. And this makes it very difficult for countries such as Argentina to benefit from free trade. Natural resources tend to have duty-free access to the markets of developed countries, but only in unprocessed form. Textile exports are constrained by complex multifibre agreements that have the purpose and effect of limiting their exports. And the labour that is unemployed in developing countries has great difficulty getting into developed-country labour markets, where advanced skills could readily be acquired. So there is a fundamental asymmetry facing poorer countries, for whom the phrase 'trade not aid' is an important and legitimate sentiment. The anti-globalisation movement comprises a mixture of contradictory forces, including both those from developing countries who regard the balance of advantage to be fundamentally unfair to their interest – an argument with which we authors have considerable

## WILL THE EURO BRING UPHEAVAL?

Ireland adopted the euro as its currency in January 1999, but the advent of euro notes and coins in January 2002 rekindled debate about the implications of abandoning our national currency. Some apocalyptic visions of what lies in store for Ireland were based on comparisons with the upheavals in Argentina following the collapse of its currency peg to the US dollar. Here is an example:

> 'The euro is part of a design to extinguish freedom in a European empire. The introduction of euro notes and coins will bring home to the Irish people that the Rubicon was crossed nine years ago [with the ratification of the Maastricht Treaty] ... Ireland really did sell its birthright for a mess of pottage. It sold itself into euro slavery that day. Now the euro notes, tokens of bondage, are here.
>
> 'It's ironic that this final humiliation should come just a few days after Argentina was reduced to riots, 27 deaths, debt default and a state of siege.
>
> '*What Argentina is suffering now, Ireland will very likely suffer over the next two or three years.*'
>
> Bernard Connolly, 'Don't throw away hard-won freedom to a Euro-superstate', *The Irish Times*, 31 December 2001 (Italics added)

These predictions can be tested against the outcome over the next two or three years! They are most unlikely to be proved correct because the differences between Ireland in the eurozone and Argentina's dollar currency board are enormous. Ireland's external debt is tiny compared with Argentina's, our banking system is sound, and our economic ties with Europe much closer than Argentina's with the US. There is no risk of the Irish public being denied access to their bank accounts, which is what triggered the political collapse in Argentina. But TV pictures of looting mobs in Buenos Aires are good for scaremongering among those worried about the soundness of the new currency.

sympathy – and those who oppose 'cheap' imports from developing countries, thereby in effect supporting a continuation of discrimination against poorer countries, a line of logic with which we have considerably less sympathy.

If globalisation is to endure and evolve as a positive force – and for Ireland it is vital that it does – it is important that the unfairness of the system to poorer countries be addressed. And this poses particular challenges for Ireland, where, via the European Union, we are relatively dependent on an agricultural support system that simultaneously denies non-EU access to European markets, and provides export refunds that undermines international markets for developing countries. The intensity and magnitude of these destructive policies for poor countries have been mitigated in recent years, and it is important that progress be continued in this regard.[3]

The challenge is to persuade the electorate and ultimately the politicians that the strategy of globalisation is the right one for the long run. Ammunition is available from the evidence that open economies weather recessions better than closed ones. Ireland's own experience in the 1950s, when relatively small external shocks led to prolonged recession, illustrates the point: Ireland's inward-looking economy stagnated longer than did economies that were more closely integrated into the global economy. The lessons from this experience need to be brought out now more than ever before in order to persuade the public to hold its nerve in the face of the hopefully short-lived spillovers from the current global recession.

# CHAPTER 5

# Population and Immigration

In Chapter 3 we saw that there are two types of growth – intensive and extensive. Intensive growth – getting more out of a given quantum of inputs, especially labour – is crucial to the growth of living standards in the long run. In this chapter we address the question of how much extensive growth is desirable. This raises some fundamental philosophical issues that are rarely debated in Ireland.

For every Irish generation since 1845, unemployment at home and emigration abroad have been facts of life, with the corollary of a falling population. At its best, emigration liberates from constraint, poverty, homogeneity, and economic and cultural inhibition; it provides opportunities to obtain new skills, widens tolerance of difference and enriches the spirit. At its worst, it can be a passage to alienation, frustration, and disintegration. Whether the experience is good or bad depends, fundamentally, on the endowments, attitudes and aptitudes emigrants take to their new home, and the scope of opportunities and cultural encouragement and acceptance they find there. But for this generation, the tide is reversed. Having imposed ourselves on the rest of the world for centuries, we now find ourselves in the unaccustomed role of hosts, with low unemployment and high in-migration. It is clear that there is considerable cultural ambivalence; the reality and potential for racial antagonisms lurks.

The context of the present debate is an economy that grew at an average annual rate of 8% for almost a decade, with almost half of this growth due to factors whose contribution is now tapering off and less than half due to rising productivity per person at work.

Here we ask the infrequently-posed question: should policy aim to maximise growth in total GDP, with its large component of extensive growth? Or should it focus more narrowly on promoting intensive growth, that is, raising the productivity and living standards of the existing population? This would include any projected labour-force growth from domestic sources. In particular, should the reality of a fall in the rate of growth of employment and the prospect of a slower rate of growth of output be a cause for concern?

In addressing this question, some international perspectives are helpful. As we saw in Chapter 3, during the 1990s the percentage increase in employment in Ireland was almost 2.7 times that of the next-best performing economy, the Netherlands, and four to five times those of Sweden, Norway, Denmark and Belgium.[1] Even more remarkably, it was double the growth of the much-vaunted US 'jobs machine'.

However, Ireland's population growth rate has been less remarkable – in fact, hardly newsworthy at all – by the standards of the United States. Between 1990 and 2000 the annual average rate of population growth in the US was 1.2% – somewhat higher than the Irish rate. But growth was unevenly spread across the regions of the US. Numerous states and cities recorded growth rates much higher than the Irish or Dublin rates.

US states which recorded much higher growth rates than Ireland were not just the sun-belt places like Nevada, Arizona and Florida, but North and South Carolina, Virginia, Delaware and so on (Figure 11). If Ireland had been a US state, its population growth rate in the 1990s would have ranked 23 out of the 50 states – between New Hampshire and Mississippi.

Almost 50 of the 280 metropolitan areas in the US grew faster than Greater Dublin in the 1990s. The expansion of Dublin was similar to that of Clarksville, Tennessee; Fresno, California; Tallahassee,

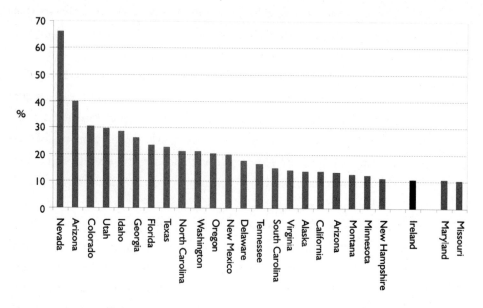

Figure 11: USA STATES' POPULATION GROWTH, 1999–2000

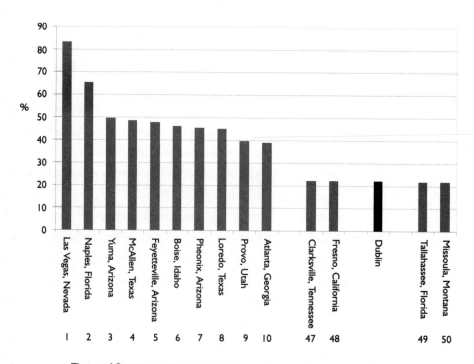

Figure 12: USA METROPOLITAN AREAS POPULATION GROWTH, 1990–2000

Florida; or Missoula, Montana (Figure 12). If we confine our attention to cities of one million or more in 1990, nine US metropolitan areas grew faster than Greater Dublin in the 1990s.

Not that we must strive to emulate the 'gold rush' cities of the US. There is a feeling that several of the fastest-growing centres – Atlanta and Seattle, for instance – would have benefited from a slower, more controlled expansion. Just like Ireland in the 1990s, the established citizens of these cities bemoan the soaring house prices, urban sprawl and endless traffic congestion that have accompanied their success.

Should we aspire to grow as fast as a booming US region or metropolitan area? What do we gain from trying to grow the economy faster than is required to cope with the natural growth of population and labour force? How important is it to maintain employment growth by encouraging further increases in participation – mainly among women with young children – and/or augmenting the natural growth of the labour force by encouraging further immigration?

We have already acknowledged the enormous benefits that rapid employment growth and the achievement of full employment bestowed on the Irish economy during the 1990s. The fall in the unemployment rate and the reversal of the age-old pattern of emigration were obvious and welcome consequences. Immigration was also very beneficial from a national perspective because of its contribution to raising the employment/population ratio. Most immigrants are of working age and the investment in their basic education has been borne in their country of origin. Thus Ireland in recent years has been on the receiving instead of the sending end of a 'brain drain'.

The rise in labour-force participation rates was also generally welcome because in the past they had been depressed by the lack of job opportunities. The biggest impact was on married women, but some older men and others, who were only marginally attached to the labour force during the period of high unemployment, have been drawn back into employment by the boom.

The rising employment rate also broadened the tax base and spread the tax burden more widely – the sharp reduction in the tax burden relative to national income in Ireland since the 1980s owed much to it. And though the tax burden per person at work has fallen much less dramatically, the combination of higher gross earnings, more employed persons per household, and falling average tax rates has led to a very marked increase in living standards.

Full employment has worked as a powerful instrument of social inclusion. The proportion of households with no employed member has declined more or less in line with the falling unemployment rate. Involvement in petty illegal activities has declined as the returns to employment have risen. Household income has grown more rapidly than net income per employed person due to the increase in the number of employed persons in each household. However, many of the women who are now 'gainfully employed' have substituted work in the market place for unpaid 'home duties', including childcare. This loss is not reflected in our measure of economic well-being.

But what should our aspiration be regarding the speed of growth of the total economy? This raises the philosophical question of the optimum size of our population. Two weeks before the 1916 Rising Pádraic Pearse dreamed that 'in a free Ireland the population would expand to twenty or even thirty million' and indeed the absolute size of the population has some importance in its own right.[2] The recent spurt of economic growth provided a welcome boost to Ireland's status on the global economic scene, yet we remain a small and sparsely settled country by European standards. Across the world the higher levels of economic activity are increasingly concentrated in a limited number of major urban centres, which are larger in economic terms than the whole of Ireland. Despite the rapid growth of recent years, Ireland remains far down this economic hierarchy and we cannot yet reap all the benefits associated with large and dense centres of economic activity. A larger and richer country would also be in a better position to tackle environmental problems, provided these are assigned a high priority.

But despite these benefits, the case against further extensive economic growth should also be considered.

A basic point is that there is no clear correlation between the size of an economy, or the rate of population growth, and average living standards or the rate at which they are improving. Some of the most successful European economies in recent years have been either very small or peripheral or both – Ireland, Finland and Iceland are examples – while many giant countries with rapidly growing populations are still mired in poverty: Nigeria and India, for example. Japan, the world's second largest economy, has been relatively stagnant for the past decade.

There are important arguments against a strategy of trying to maximise economic growth when this can be achieved only by stimulating the rate of population growth. When population and employment grow as rapidly as they did in Ireland in the 1990s it is almost inevitable that there will be many negative effects on the quality of life. The most important illustrations in an Irish context are the increased traffic congestion and the fact that commuting to and from work is absorbing more time and resources, house-price inflation that is having serious adverse social effects, and the degradation of the environment due to the spillovers from poorly-

## WHAT IS THE POPULATION OPTIMUM?

'Imagine that fifty to one hundred people have to live in a given territory, England for instance. Even with very advanced technology and culture they will be unable to run railways, steel foundries, etc., and have to be content to live as craftsmen, or even as shepherds. The standard of living will be very low. If on the contrary 200 to 500 million people were to try to live on the same island they would have to cultivate even the poorest soils, usually by hand, so as to obtain the highest output per acre; the standard of living would be equally low … Between these two extremes there must be more beneficial intermediate positions. *The most beneficial of all is called the optimum.*'

Alfred Sauvy, *General Theory of Population*, Paris, 1966

(Of course, this passage ignores the role of international trade, which can substitute for a large domestic population.)

managed growth in areas ranging from waste disposal to intensive agricultural production. Finally, the economic stringency put in place in the late 1980s that facilitated the boom of the 1990s relied heavily on reductions in the public capital programme. The unanticipated employment and population boom compounded the effects of these cutbacks, with the result that many sectors are now seriously overstretched and the quality of services provided has declined sharply. As the boom gathered pace, these negative effects of growth increased more rapidly, and an awareness of their impact on the quality of life dawned belatedly.

## CONGESTION A FORM OF HIDDEN INFLATION

Longer commuting times and queues, waiting lists for housing and other services are really a form of suppressed inflation that is not reflected in the official statistics. Economists were quick to draw attention to these problems in centrally planned economies and they should now take account of their impact on the well-being of people living in the 'hot spots' of western economies.

By 2000 the Irish unemployment rate had fallen to a level generally regarded as 'full employment', labour-force participation rates were up to average European levels, and emigration had been replaced by immigration. Continued rapid growth would have generated higher wage inflation. While policy makers worried about the impact of this on the longer-term competitiveness of the economy, its immediate effect on workers' living standards is beneficial. But the pressure from a tight labour market would intensify unless measures were implemented to increase the rate of population growth. Are the benefits of this extensive growth sufficient to warrant such policies? While the current slowdown may postpone a serious consideration of this issue, it will not do so indefinitely.

It is difficult to justify subsidies to job creation in a situation where the jobs created cannot be filled from the existing labour force. Simple job creation is no longer adequate justification and other considerations have to be invoked. These include the goals of creating higher value-added (and higher-wage) jobs to be filled by existing workers moving up the job hierarchy and the belief that it is still necessary to offer incentives to certain types of projects that will bestow significant positive externalities on the economy. There may also be a continuing justification for spending public money to promote employment in regions with relatively high rates of labour-market slack. But it is likely that attracting new projects to the Dublin region will aggravate a situation that is already sub-optimal in view of growing congestion and other negative spillovers. Even allowing for the current growth pause, it is now time to exercise greater selectivity in the industrial promotion process.[3]

Of course, it is possible to argue that maximising the growth of employment remains a priority, even if it requires measures to stimulate the supply of labour. While we authors do not endorse this view, it is worth considering the type of measures that might be implemented.

Two possible approaches could be advocated to maintain the elastic supply of labour that facilitated the 1990s boom, one centring on increased domestic labour supply, the other on augmenting increased immigration.

**Domestic labour supply**: The possibility here is to consider changes in the tax system designed to increase the supply of labour from the existing population. If successful, these would facilitate faster growth in output and mitigate the effects of falling unemployment on the wage-bargaining process. But the leeway in this is not very great. The evidence suggests that the responsiveness of the labour supply to tax cuts is falling and that Ireland is now facing a situation where lower taxes will increase the disposable income of those already in the labour force but do little to increase the size of the labour force. Even if tax cuts induced the labour-force participation rates of women aged 25 to 54 to rise to the EU average, only an additional 70,000 women would join the labour force, approximately equivalent to one year's increase in employment in recent years.

75

Whatever the broader merits of increased labour-force participation, it is unlikely to offer more than short-term relief to the problem of labour shortages. But, in any event, major initiatives on this front have been incorporated in recent budgets and the debate about future policy in this area is now concerned with relatively minor adjustments.

**Immigration**: The most obvious policy available to stimulate the supply of labour is to encourage immigration. An inflow of working-age adults has many attractions as a way of supplementing the natural increase of the labour force and easing specific skill bottlenecks. But the impact of large-scale immigration on the well-being of the population has to be carefully evaluated. While the immigrants themselves may be assumed to regard residence in Ireland as an improvement on the alternatives open to them – and a valid case can be made for Irish policy makers taking this into account on humanitarian grounds – the impact of immigration on the well-being of those already resident in Ireland will remain the dominant consideration.[4]

There are narrow limits to Ireland's ability to manage sizeable inflows from other countries, especially those outside the EU. It is only realistic to acknowledge the constraint of 'absorptive capacity'. Comparisons with the ease with which the Irish were able to flood into the New World to escape poverty and discrimination at home are misplaced, most fundamentally because of the absence of even the most rudimentary welfare state at that time. Under

**CHILDCARE**

The main potential for increased labour-force participation is among women in households where young children are present and the main constraint is the availability of suitable childcare. The increased incentive for spouses to return to work due to the 'individualisation' of the tax system raises the demand for these services and, in the short run at least, results in higher costs rather than increased availability.

contemporary Irish conditions uncontrolled immigration would be a recipe for social tension and conflict, especially in the inner-city areas where the newcomers are most likely to congregate. Specific issues are raised by the fact that infants born in Ireland along with their parents gain automatic Irish citizenship. To cope successfully with large-scale immigration would require investing significant resources in the housing, education, and training of immigrants. Failure to do so would threaten the social consensus on which the welfare state is built. An open-door policy by Ireland would, in any event, trouble our EU partners – immigration policy is another area where we are no longer sovereign. But the point that must not be lost sight of is that advocacy of increased immigration should be linked to explicit proposals for handling the associated costs.

More generally, policies designed to sustain extensive growth of the economy should be evaluated taking account of the adverse spillovers and other costs associated with that type of growth.

## Public Attitudes to Emigrants

In a survey of 1500 adults carried out by the Urban Institute in UCD, each respondent was asked whether she or he personally had a positive or negative attitude towards people from specific minority ethnic groups. These groups included: Irish Travellers, Chinese, Black African/Caribbean and Eastern European. Significantly, respondents were more than twice as likely to suggest that they held either a 'negative' or 'very negative' attitude towards Irish Travellers than Chinese (37% and 15% respectively). Just under a quarter of respondents stated their view of Black African/Caribbean people and Eastern Europeans as either 'negative' or 'very negative' (23% and 22%). Members of the Chinese community were most likely to be perceived positively, with just under two-thirds (65%) saying that this group was seen 'very positively' (8%) or 'positively' (57%). Travellers engendered more negative attitudes than any of the immigrant groups.

**Table 3**

**Personal Attitude to Minority Groups**

|  | Irish Travellers | Chinese | Black African/ Caribbean | Eastern Europeans |
|---|---|---|---|---|
|  | % | % | % | % |
| Very Positive | 8 | 8 | 7 | 8 |
| Positive | 45 | 57 | 44 | 47 |
| Negative | 28 | 11 | 18 | 16 |
| Very Negative | 9 | 4 | 7 | 6 |
| Don't Know | 11 | 20 | 24 | 23 |

More than half of people in all geographical areas viewed the settlement of minority groups in their area as being acceptable. There was a more positive attitude among those in small towns.

## Lessons for the Future

It is important to emphasise that Ireland has benefited greatly from the recent change from emigration to immigration. Being able to provide jobs for those of our young people who want to live in Ireland is a very welcome novelty, while the energy, talent, innovation and commitment that 'blow-ins' bring to a hospitable community yield many dividends, including economic and social vitality, reduction in the pressures of wage inflation, and, in some cases – e.g. nurses recruited from the Philippines, farm workers recruited from the Baltic countries – averting collapse in key sectors. We should highlight the various facets of this contribution and let the public know how important it has been and continues to be for our well-being.

But the booming economy increased this influx to the point that Ireland has the highest rate of net immigration in Europe, which has added to the inflation in the housing market and to traffic congestion,

**Table 4**

**Acceptability of Minority Groups Locally by Area (%)**

| | Dublin City | Other City | Large Town (pop=10,000–40,000) | Small Town (pop=1–10,000) | Village/ Rural/ Open Area |
|---|---|---|---|---|---|
| Very Acceptable | 6.5 | 14.7 | 12.9 | 12.2 | 6.9 |
| Acceptable | 58.3 | 49.1 | 54.0 | 63.5 | 49.8 |
| Not Very Acceptable | 19.1 | 19.0 | 18.4 | 12.2 | 20.4 |
| Not At All Acceptable | 6.7 | 6.7 | 1.2 | 2.7 | 5.6 |
| Don't Know | 9.4 | 10.4 | 13.5 | 9.5 | 17.3 |

and the emergence of overt and not so overt racism in some quarters. A continuation of influx at this rate is likely to intensify these problems and in the worst case result in an atmosphere that makes immigrants feel unwelcome, with all the personal costs that this engenders for those involved, and the losses to our economy and social life which will be incurred if people of commitment and energy are inhibited from contributing because of hostility.

The slow-down in the economy provides us with an opportunity to develop a more coherent approach to this sensitive issue. In doing so, Ireland has to recognise that its freedom of manoeuvre with regard to immigration is constrained by our EU commitments and the goal of adopting an EU-wide common policy on immigration and asylum seekers by the year 2005. Within these constraints, what sort of an immigration policy do we advocate here?

The answer is a policy that minimises the adverse spillovers associated with large-scale immigration and maximises the benefits to the Irish economy of the inflow. We should set a realistic ceiling on the numbers permitted to enter the country. It is unrealistic to ignore the limits on the country's immigration absorptive capacity. More generally, there is little merit in encouraging higher population inflows simply to maximise the growth of GDP. Living standards depend on

79

## THE 'BLOW-IN' FACTOR IN WEST CORK

'West Cork has become a favourite place for new faces to settle and to prosper. Tony Settle (English, former creative director in Asia and Europe of Leo Burnett, one of the world's leading advertising agencies) and his wife Alicia (Singaporean Chinese, expert in Chinese foods and herbal teas) bought a 150-acre farm (Bunalon) in West Cork in 1994. They have no Irish links, and chose Cork because it has "pure air straight from the Atlantic". They have developed a range of herbal teas that are shipped all over the world, and a variety of specialist organic products that are sold both locally (directly) and are on the shelves in Selfridges and Fortnum & Mason. Tony is quoted as follows: "It's all about flavour. Bunalun isn't austerity organic, it's gourmet organic. We're passionate about organic because we want our food to taste terrific. So far as possible, we grow all our own ingredients, pick them when they're perfect, and then go from field to jar the same day to capture every bit of flavour."'

The Observer Food Monthly, 14 October 2001, p.48

GDP per person, and arguably the most important measure is GDP per head of existing population.

The corollary to this strategy is to make every effort to ensure that those who enter are encouraged and facilitated in every way to become full and contributing members of the Irish community. The benefits from immigration can be maximised by trying to ensure that the immigrants are quickly assimilated into the job market, rather than, as tends to be case under present policies towards asylum seekers, educated in the finer points of the welfare system. The worst outcome is a system that encourages an inflow of immigrants but places obstacles in their path to legitimate employment, deflecting them instead into dependency on welfare and illegal activities.

Even though the survey results presented in this chapter suggest a generally positive attitude to minority groups, as the country encounters recession it is likely that social pressure will intensify to discriminate against those foreigners already at work here. Those of us who have had the privilege of working abroad understand the feelings of vulnerability that assailed us when the host economy went into recession and unemployment rose. And we also know how grateful we were when, in spite of these stresses, we were encouraged to stay and continue making our contribution. The Psalmist tells us that 'the stone which the builders rejected became the corner stone'. The least amongst us can become the greatest when we are treated with dignity and respect.

An important but less obvious point is that trying to fine-tune the immigrant stream to meet skill shortages in the domestic economy is not necessarily the wisest policy. It is impossible to predict the supply–demand balance by occupation even a few years ahead. This year's skill shortages have a nasty habit of becoming next year's over-crowded occupations. Market forces steer people into the areas where they earn the highest returns, but they must also be prepared to redirect their efforts, retrain and relocate, especially early in their careers. Only through this process can the needs of a dynamic, changing economy be met fairly smoothly. The implication is that the most desirable traits in the immigrant stream are self-reliance and a commitment to hard work, rather than specific educational qualifications. The futility of trying to channel immigration flows into specific

**OPEN BORDERS?**

'The present Irish policy, like that of most other European countries, is to recruit immigrants with advanced skills, especially in information technology. This may, however, be short-sighted. One of the few predictions I would venture to make is that in ten or twenty years there will be throughout Europe a plethora of computer specialists and the like, and the real shortages will be in the traditional service trades – carpenters, home helps, plumbers, common nurse and so on. Ireland is better placed than most other EU countries to follow an open door policy in line with the words on the American Statue of Liberty:

Give me your tired, your poor,
Your huddled masses yearning to be free.'

Journalist and economic commentator Samuel Brittan, Davy conference on the future of the euro, Dublin, 1 December 2000 sectors and occupations has been illustrated by recent flip-flops in Irish policy – at one time sending delegations far afield to recruit computer programmers, then imposing tighter restrictions on employers who wish to employ immigrants. Within the guidelines set out above, a *laissez-faire* approach is best. The removal of obstacles to self-employment in occupations that have been traditional routes to assimilation and advancement by immigrants – from taxi driving to running convenience stores – should be actively pursued as part of our national immigration policy.

# CHAPTER 6

# Economic Policy Responses

One of the drivers of the rapid expansion of the late 1990s was the weakness of the euro and the fall in real interest rates. These developments were favourable shocks that followed from Ireland's adoption of the euro. They ensured a continued export boom, a strong inflow of FDI and rapid productivity growth in the manufacturing sector. But they also generated inflationary pressures as labour shortages became more acute and employees exercised their increasing bargaining power to obtain wage increases that outstripped productivity growth.

Ireland's inflation rate reached twice the eurozone average during 2000 (Figure 13). This outcome would hardly have been thought possible at the time we adopted the single currency, when it was widely anticipated that membership of the eurozone would ensure that our inflation rate would remain very close to that of the continental economies. We are now aware that, even in a monetary union, domestic pressures remain a significant influence on inflation. And as a consequence of the inflationary impact of the fall in the euro since January 1999 we are also more conscious of the degree to which entry to the eurozone placed Ireland in an anomalous situation due to the low proportion of our trade that is with the other members of the monetary union. However, the decline in the Irish inflation rate – both absolutely and relative to the eurozone rate – in the course of

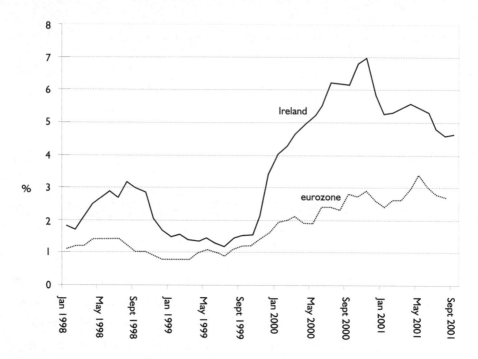

Figure 13: IRISH AND EUROZONE INFLATION

2001 has renewed the prospect that over the medium term the inflation differentials between member states will be minor.

Following the publication of Budget 2001 early in December 2000, a marked divergence of views emerged between those (including the EU Commission and many academic economists in Ireland and abroad) who deemed it inappropriate under current Irish macro-economic conditions to introduce a budget that was broadly expansionary and those (including the Minister for Finance and some Irish commentators) who believed either that the budget was not in any meaningful sense expansionary or that the supply-side effects of lower income-tax rates would offset the stimulus to demand. Some have gone further to argue that Irish fiscal policy is largely irrelevant, having little impact on Irish inflation and no impact on the euro, implying that tax and spending plans should be framed largely with regard to the public sector's current and capital requirements and an acceptable burden of taxation.

## THE VIEW FROM CAMBRIDGE, MASSACHUSETTS

'In announcing the budget for 2001, the [Irish] government has just delivered on an earlier promise of income-tax cuts. This has led to a revision by the Central Bank of its forecast of CPI inflation for 2001 from 4% to 5% and a forecast of wage inflation of 9.75%.

'These tax cuts have been part of an original combination, tax cuts in exchange for wage moderation in 2001, within the structure of the agreement known as the PPF. This way, the government has argued, the economy will continue to grow and grow without wage inflation.

'Does this particular form of incomes policy make sense? From a distance, not much – not in the current economic situation facing Ireland. The claim that the income-tax cuts will increase labour supply and thus allow for a further decrease in equilibrium unemployment is implausible. At best, this tax cut plus wage moderation will buy time. But sooner or later the economy will have to slow down, and this will require a wage increase or/and a fiscal contraction.'

Olivier Blanchard, 'Country Adjustments within Euroland. Lessons after Two Years', in 'Monitoring the European Central Bank', CEPR, London, March 2001

The sustainability of growth at the rate recorded in the late 1990s arises from the link between the growth of output and employment on the one hand, and the unemployment rate on the other. Despite the elastic labour supply Ireland enjoyed during the 1990s, there has been a stable relationship between the growth of output and reductions in the unemployment rate. GDP growth in excess of 4.5% triggers a fall in the unemployment rate. The historical record suggests that for every percentage point growth above this, the unemployment rate falls by about one third of a percentage point. Increasing the rate of growth of the labour force can alter the link: a policy of encouraging immigration and increased labour-force participation should make it possible to sustain a higher growth rate without further falls in the unemployment rate. But over the years the relationship between growth and unemployment has been surprisingly stable.

The implication is that as the Irish economy continued to grow for

**THE VIEW FROM LONDON**

'Higher wages may seem an odd way of reducing demand, but in a fixed-exchange rate system they are the only way to reduce the super-competitiveness that fuels excess demand. The PPF has been remarkably successful in restraining wages and keeping Ireland competitive. It was the right policy when Ireland had abundant unemployed labour but has reached the end of its useful life.'

*Financial Times* editorial, London, 8 December 2000

a few more years at 7% to 10% the unemployment rate fell to extremely low levels, leading to an increasingly difficult labour-market situation from the employers' perspective and an intensification of the inflationary pressures that were already building up in the labour market. If external factors had remained favourable, the continued rapid expansion of the economy would have become self-defeating as the labour market overheated. Even as the economy slowed down towards the end of 2001, the unemployment rate remained very low and inflationary pressures in the labour market remained high. The logic of a link between the growth of output and the level of unemployment is that only after the GDP growth rate has been below 4.5% for some time will there be a significant rise in the unemployment rate. In a very optimistic scenario – a quick rebound in the world economy – we could be spared this outcome.

Changes in interest rates are now the main instrument for stabilising the economy in the US and other advanced economies. Ireland relinquished monetary and exchange-rate policy to the European Central Bank by adopting the euro in 1999. The result of this was a two-fold stimulus to the economy due to (i) the sharp decline of the euro relative to sterling and the dollar, which far outweigh the euro in terms of their importance to Irish trade, and (ii) the fall in interest rates in the late 1990s due to the convergence of eurozone rates. An independent Irish Central Bank would have raised interest rates in the late 1990s to cool the housing market. If

## LOW MULTIPLIERS ARE NOT ZERO

Disillusion with the excesses of fiscal policy in the late 1970s led many Irish economists to promulgate an over-simplified version of the 'small open economy' textbook model of the impact of fiscal policy. This model was used to discredit the cruder Keynesian models of earlier decades, according to which the government could work wonders for the level of output and employment through relatively small injections to the stream of aggregate demand. The revisionist argument went that since Ireland is such a small and open economy, most extra spending 'leaks' abroad in the form of higher imports, so the multiplier is very low. This debunked the idea that we enjoyed multipliers of 4 or 5, which are still used to illustrate the theory in many US textbooks. A more realistic value would be in the region of 1, but it could be higher or lower depending on whether the stimulus takes the form of tax cuts for the lower paid, or increased spending on roads, and so on. But a low multiplier is not a zero multiplier – even if the multiplier is 'only' 1, then an injection of €100 million into the economy would raise the equilibrium level of output by €100 million – assuming the economy is not constrained by labour shortages or other supply-side limits.

Despite the decline in popularity of the Keynesian model among academic economists in the US, there has been surprising support there for both fiscal and monetary stimulus as a response to the current slowdown. We are all reborn as Keynesians during a recession!

the exchange rate had continued to float as it did between 1993 and 1998 the Irish pound would now almost certainly be much higher relative to sterling and the dollar than it is as a sub-currency of euro. These monetary/exchange-rate moves would have had a moderating effect on our growth rate. The unavailability of these instruments was a major constraint on Irish policy in the late 1990s, but now that the economy has slowed, conditions in Ireland have come more into line with those in the eurozone on which the European Central Bank bases it policies.

Fiscal policy – changes in the balance between government

## HOW REGIONS ADJUST TO ADVERSE SHOCKS

It is fashionable to compare Ireland to a booming region, capable of much faster growth than a large country because of the openness of its labour and capital markets. However, regions too have to adjust to shocks, as outlined here by Mark Wynne:

'The Texas recession of the 1980s was a classic example of an asymmetric shock. Texas did not have the option of devaluing ... so the adjustment occurred by other means. Out-migration was an important part of this process ... [An inflow of over 2.5% a year turned into an outflow of almost 1% a year.] When a state's real economic circumstances change, real adjustments have to occur, sooner or later ...'

Mark Wynne, Federal Reserve Bank of Dallas, at the Davy Conference on EMU, Dublin, 1 December 2000

revenue and spending – is the other pillar of macroeconomic policy. It has been used sparingly in the major economies in recent times. The orthodox view is that we should allow 'automatic stabilisers' to work – that is, tax revenues to fall and social welfare payments to rise as the economy moves into recession – but not to use changes in tax rates and spending to try to fine tune the economy. The way the Irish budget surplus exceeded forecasts during the late 1990s is a good illustration of automatic stabilisers at work – higher than expected surpluses acted a brake on the economy, while the dramatic under-shooting of the projected surplus in 2001 reversed this trend. However, the EU Stability and Growth Pact, which forces governments to cap deficits at 3%, may perversely limit the operation of these stabilisers. France and Germany risk violating the pact as their economies falter. It is to be hoped that the EU would re-examine the pact should this happen, just as the deepening downturn in the US economy and the shock of 11 September 2001 prompted conservative policy makers to propose a fiscal stimulus.

Despite the loss of an independent currency and the constraints imposed by the Stability Pact, the Irish authorities still retain some room for independent fiscal policy. But independence has not been wisely exercised. Fiscal policy has tended to be 'pro-cyclical' – that is, leaning with rather than against the wind. The most recent assessment concludes that 'the last five budgets, 1997–2001, with the exception of 2000, have all been expansionary in their impact, imparting a cumulative stimulus of over 3 percentage points of GDP

## BUDGETARY POLICY

The budget of December 2000 was given low marks by most macroeconomic commentators, especially the Commission of the EU. The fall in the cyclically adjusted budget surplus – a sophisticated measure of the stance of fiscal policy – was regarded as inappropriate for an economy already strained by labour shortages and other bottlenecks. The desire to alleviate bottlenecks by massive increases in the public capital programme risked making matters worse rather than better, in the short run at least. The Minister justified his approach by claiming that 'Ireland is different' and that the economic constraints could be overcome by his unconventional approach. This theme was absent from his budget in December 2001.

to the economy.'[1] In particular, it was widely believed – and not just by the EU Commission – that the December 2000 budget gave too much away in tax cuts and pumped too much extra spending into an economy that was growing at breakneck speed. As the economy slowed during 2001 these concerns faded, and, indeed, some argued that the December 2001 budget could have imparted more stimulus to the economy in order to minimise the impact of the recession.

## Lessons for the Future

Lefty Gomez, the American baseball player, is quoted as saying: 'I'd rather be lucky than good.' We've been very lucky, in that, in a full employment economy, we have followed an expansionary fiscal policy that could have been expected to lead to rising inflation in the price of services and associated wages, and a further overheating of the property market. Instead, like the *deus ex machina* that comes from the sky in Greek plays and solves the unresolved by divine intervention, an emerging recession and the Twin Towers cataclysm makes such a policy now seem well judged and appropriate. Domestic demand has been stimulated as global demand slows. But it is important that Ireland does not exhaust its capacity to use fiscal measures to correct for global dysfunction at this point, and leave itself with no remaining capacity to respond if hit with exchange-rate difficulties.

It is essential that during a downturn policy makers avoid any pro-cyclical measures such as raising taxes, but, given the fundamental soundness of the public finances (as evidenced by surpluses of the last five years, the falling debt/GDP ratio, and interest rates that are negative in real terms), there is no need for panic in the face of a sharp but temporary deterioration in the public finances. The accelerated programme of expenditure on infrastructure proposed in the National Development Plan should be maintained. On the tax side, the budgetary stance should be largely neutral, with the tax structure adjusted to allow for inflation. While further generous tax cuts would obviously be inappropriate, significant discretionary tax increases are not required.

If neutrality is achieved on the tax side of the budget, the growth of expenditure should also be broadly in line with inflation. Assuming indexation of social-welfare benefits and a falling burden of debt service, the missing piece of the puzzle is the level of spending on the public-sector wage bill. There are strong pressures to increase the numbers in the public services and their rates of pay. These pressures constitute the greatest threat to implementing an appropriate budgetary strategy over the medium term. The problem is highlighted by the rapid increase in current spending (excluding national debt interest) in recent years. But, despite rapid increases in the public-sector wage bill, the pressure for higher pay and increased numbers persists. It is clear that the traditional 'partnership' approach has not been able to contain pay levels in the public sector. A process has evolved whereby groups regard the pay increases negotiated in the national agreements as only a starting point. So, a discussion of budgetary policy leads naturally to the topic of pay policy.

**Pay policy**: As we have noted, the exceptional growth of the late 1990s was fuelled by several external stimuli, the most important being the booming US economy, the weak euro and negative real interest rates. Rapid growth drove unemployment to a very low level and low unemployment fuelled higher wage inflation, leading to some loss of competitiveness. These developments were among the reasons for the slow-down in Irish growth already noticeable by early 2001. Rising relative costs – especially labour costs – are the most important way of balancing aggregate supply and demand and moving the economy to the lower growth rate that is sustainable over the longer run. As Olivier Blanchard argues in the box on p.85, wage inflation was part of the solution to the Irish predicament in 2000 rather than a new problem. But the danger now is that wages will overshoot the level required to restore balance between supply and demand in the labour market. The temporary fall in demand due to the global recession implies a fall in the equilibrium wage rate just as actual wage levels are rising rapidly in response to historical tight labour-market conditions.

Until 2001 the rapid growth of productivity in manufacturing more than offset the rise in wage costs, as shown in the Central Bank's index of competitiveness, which improved in 2000. However, this index is confined to the manufacturing sector and takes no account of unfavourable developments on other fronts, such as increasing congestion and capacity constraints. It is also strongly influenced by the exceptional performance of a few high-tech sectors. None the less, it shows that up to the time of the current downturn in global economic activity, wage inflation had not seriously eroded the economy's competitiveness or its attractiveness as a location for inward foreign investment. But the index stabilised in 2001 as higher wage inflation and a stronger exchange rate took their toll. The long period of steady competitive gains appears to have come to an end.

In looking at the role of the 'national partnership' in the contemporary industrial relations scene it is often not adequately recognised that this approach owed its origins to the crisis level of unemployment that prevailed as late as 1993. The labour-market situation has been completely transformed in the interim. Both employers and employees face very different incentives in pay bargaining now than they did ten years ago. As labour shortages become more acute, employees increasingly exercise their market power to extract larger wage increases. In the public sector employees are increasingly unwilling to trade off higher pay for security of employment. Employers with buoyant demand for their output are facing ever-stronger incentives to accede to high wage claims. Increases in take-home pay due to tax cuts do not remove these incentives. A rising rate of wage inflation is required to restore the balance between supply and demand.

And, in fact, in every year since 1988 nominal wage growth exceeded the terms of the National Wage Agreement (NWA) – in some years by a very significant margin. Moreover, this excess wage inflation was not needed to compensate for unexpected price infla-tion – the rate of increase in real wages also exceeded what was pro-vided for in the NWAs by on average over 3% a year.[2] The failure of the agreements to hit their targets during the 1990s presumably reflected the tightening labour market, as did the speed with which the PPF was renegotiated to incorporate higher-than-anticipated inflation in 2000. But it is unlikely that deterioration in the economic situation would be as quickly reflected in a downward adjustment in basic wage inflation. This asymmetry is a serious flaw in the process.

Many economists are sceptical about the desirability of trying to enforce a national wage agreement in a fully-employed economy. The alternative of allowing wages to rise in an uncoordinated manner is the norm in other countries. It has the merit of allowing increasing wage differentials to allocate labour to the most productive sectors. Highly profitable companies can outbid less profitable ones in the competition for employees. This helps to direct the economy's scarce resources towards their most efficient uses. However, this is achieved at the cost of higher negotiation and information costs, and possibly a loss of industrial peace. The reduced effectiveness of the most recent agreement – the Partnership for Prosperity and Fairness (PPF) – in delivering industrial peace, especially in the public sector, combined with ever-increasing comprehensiveness of these agreements, suggests that the whole approach may have outlived its usefulness. We authors understand the logic of linking wage arguments with tax cuts so as to arrive at a take-home pay target. But the gradual accretion of other issues within these agreements has had a number of unwelcome effects. The range of interests involved in the PPF negotiations (see box below) suggests that the objectives extended far beyond the basic goal of promoting industrial peace and keeping the economy competitive to include 'bringing about a fairer and more inclusive Ireland' and 'promoting an entrepreneurial culture'. This has exacerbated the 'insider-outsider' problem, whereby some key centres of influence besides employers and unions are involved, but inevitably many are not. And the problem is that those who are allowed to gather around the national Christmas tree can get their baubles hung, while these are paid for in part by those outside the magic circle. The citizenry have little idea what is being negotiated, ostensibly on their behalf, and even fewer know what has been agreed. There is no necessary association between the general public interest and the agglomeration of

**PARTICIPANTS IN THE PARTNERSHIP FOR PROSPERITY AND FAIRNESS**

The parties to the PPF negotiations included the Government, employers, trade unions, farmers and the community and voluntary sector as follows: Irish Business and Employers' Confederation (IBEC), Irish Congress of Trade Unions (ICTU), Construction Industry Federation (CIF), Irish Farmers' Association (IFA), Irish Creamery Milk Suppliers' Association (ICMSA), Irish Co-Operative Organisation Society Ltd. (ICOS), Macra na Feirme, Irish National Organisation of the Unemployed (INOU), Congress Centres for the Unemployed, The Community Platform, Conference of Religious of Ireland (CORI), National Women's Council of Ireland (NWCI), National Youth Council of Ireland (NYCI), Society of Saint Vincent de Paul, Protestant Aid, Small Firms' Association (SFA), Irish Exporters' Association (IEA), Irish Tourist Industry Confederation (ITIC) and Chambers of Commerce of Ireland (CCI).

selected individual interests. In a time of adversity it is no longer appropriate to seek to resolve a very wide range of economic and social issues in this manner. We must now question the whole approach.

It is now relevant to question not only the effectiveness of this approach but also its appropriateness. In an open economy, without a separate exchange rate or monetary policy, increases in nominal rates of pay that are not justified by productivity gains will affect the level of employment. Unwarranted wage inflation will lead to job losses and either a resumption of emigration or higher unemployment. So too will external shocks of the type that Ireland experienced in the course of 2001. Increased wage flexibility has an important role to play in minimising the social and economic costs of adjustment under these circumstances. In the rapidly changing environment now facing the social partners we believe that employers and employees should welcome the prospect of a return to decentralised pay bargaining.

But it is possible to envisage modifying the social partnership approach to retain its benefits – principally in terms of minimising the resources that have to be devoted to wage bargaining at the level of the firm – while at the same time achieving increased labour-market flexibility. Several proposals have been made – such as the use of contingency-based contracts that would allow renegotiation of the wage terms in the event of shocks such as sterling depreciation or a global recession.

Our bottom line is that continuation of the social partnership approach in the changed circumstances of the Irish economy is attractive only on two conditions:

➤ That the ambitious and increasingly inclusive 'social engineering' accretions to the basic wage agreement be scrapped. Pay policy should not be linked to the wide range of social policy issues that have become incorporated in the national wage agreements over the years.

➢ That a significant element of flexibility be incorporated into the basic agreement, to allow some automatic adjustment of the rate of pay increase as the economic context changes. The simplest way of doing this might be to link wage inflation directly to the rate of unemployment, but other formulae have been proposed. The case for such flexibility becomes compelling if we are confronted by a sustained recession and associated rising unemployment. We can assume that the flexibility provisions as regards individual companies will be availed of in the private sector by employers and unions to allow downward adjustments to meet new market realities. But if such flexibility were not characteristic in the public sector, and growth in real public-sector wages and salaries were occurring while the total pool of resources contracted, then well-being would suffer as public-sector Peter could only be paid for at the expense of private-sector Paul.

# CHAPTER 7

# Spatial Strategy

Although the island of Ireland can meaningfully be regarded as a region of the larger EU economy, the interest in the regional distribution of economic activity within the country remains high. Policy makers are continually faced with the question, explicitly or implicitly: How much national economic growth should be traded off for a better 'regional balance'?

Here, we take a very broad view of the regional question, distinguishing only between the Greater Dublin region (Dublin + Mideast) and the rest of the State. (We are not persuaded of the advantage of having regional authorities in areas that vary in population from 1.5

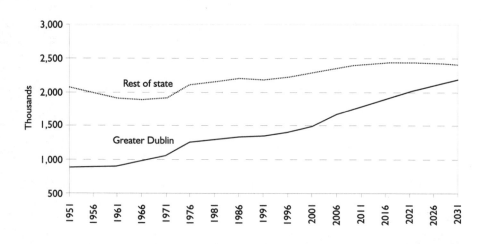

Figure 14: REGIONAL POPULATION GROWTH

million in Greater Dublin to just over 200,000 in the Midland region.) Figure 14 shows the historical and projected future growth of the national population, broken down simply between the Greater Dublin region and the rest of the State. The inexorable growth of the Greater Dublin region is the main feature. Regional policy has failed to alter this, although in recent years the absolute decline of the rest of the State has been halted. But the trend that many will no doubt find disturbing is brought out in Figure 15, showing the rising share of the national population in Greater Dublin.

The dynamics of the present population structure play a large role in these trends. The natural increase of the population in Greater Dublin is much higher than in the peripheral regions. But this is reinforced by migration within the State and also into the State – in recent years the Greater Dublin region has been the only net gainer from internal migration and by far the largest recipient of migration to the State. These forces imply that by the fourth decade of this century almost half the population of the country will be living in Greater Dublin. Such a concentration of population would be exceptional by

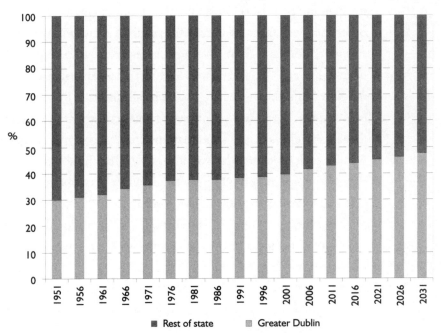

Figure 15: REGIONAL POPULATION SHARES

European standards. The projected increase of a further 50% in the population of Greater Dublin is comparable to that recorded over the past thirty years – to which we have not yet adjusted. The scale of the challenge is daunting. On the other hand, the population of the rest of the country is likely to grow by only about 10% over the same period. Coping with the infrastructural needs of the rest of the country, where a pattern of low-density, dispersed settlement is likely to continue to prevail, is also a daunting prospect.

National population projections are notoriously uncertain – and regional projections even more so. A sharp recession leading to the resumption of net emigration would render these projections useless, just as most of the attempts published in the 1970s to quantify 'Ireland in the Year 2000' proved very wide of the mark. None the less, we have to face up to the likelihood that as the growth of population slows it will become more concentrated in the Greater Dublin region.

Regional policy attempts to change the distribution of population and economic activity from what would occur without intervention. This can be justified in order to achieve certain social goals, such as maintaining population in rural areas, and reducing congestion and other spillovers from the excessive growth of a few large urban areas. But it is difficult to point to many instances where such goals have been achieved. The forces that lead to agglomeration are strong – modern firms like to cluster geographically in order to be near deep labour markets and sub-supply sectors. Draconian interference with these preferences entails a cost in terms of slower growth. A key question for policy makers is how much overall growth should we be prepared to sacrifice in the hope of achieving a growth pattern that is believed to be fairer or more balanced?

In answering this question, our policy makers should not forget the relative smallness of the Irish economy. We discussed this point previously, in Chapter 5. Not only is Ireland a small country, its largest metropolitan area is also small by international standards. Moreover, Dublin's growth rate has not been that exceptional in an international perspective. Thinking of Ireland as a region of a larger

**CHANGING CIRCUMSTANCES AFFECT HOUSE PRICES**

The recent deterioration in Britain's public transport system – the railways in particular – is reported to be having a marked affect on relative house prices. Prices in the outer commuter belt – towns that were within 60 to 90 minutes of London by train – have fallen as the speed restrictions on the rail network lengthen travel times. Housing closer to the city has risen in value.

According to the September 2000 household survey, over half of Ireland's workforce now travels to work by car – and three-quarters of these do not carry any passengers.

economy – a perspective prompted by our close integration into the EU and adoption of the euro as our currency – we recalled that many states of the US, for example, recorded much higher growth rates than Ireland during the 1990s. Similarly, a comparison of Greater Dublin with the metropolitan areas of the US shows that that almost 50 of the 280 US metropolitan areas grew faster than Greater Dublin in the 1990s. Some of these US cities grew faster than their inhabitants would have wished and in areas like Seattle, Washington; Portland, Oregon; and Atlanta, Georgia, some policies to discourage further development were implemented. None the less, these comparisons suggest that it is not impossible to cope with the pace of growth recorded in Ireland and Dublin in the 1990s.

## Lessons for the Future

Dublin remains relatively small in international terms, and its growth rates are likewise not exceptional in a North American context. The organic growth it has experienced and is likely to experience in the future, will not yield easily to policy, and any policies directed at radically changing this could damage not just the Dublin region but the country as a whole.

The Dublin experience demonstrates that scale is important, that agglomeration and economic vitality are related to size. This argues the case for the 'gateway' strategy, the encouragement in the country of a few other nodes that have some chance of competing with the Dublin region.

The regional strategy – if the current lines on maps can be so characterised – suffers from two serious and debilitating limitations. First, in a global competitive context, the designated regions outside Dublin are too small, and secondly, they have no public identity. No one wears a jersey for the Midlands region. There are two credible choices:

Treat the country as two regions – Dublin and the Rest of Ireland. This would give the latter economic and demographic parity, and could engender serious competition for the former.

The second is to use the four provinces – Connacht, Ulster, Munster and Leinster – as the fulcrums for institutional and economic development. We understand the pragmatic logic of designating the Border Midlands and West (BMW) region to come within the income thresholds so as to draw down the last substantive EU cohesion funding likely to be available to Ireland. (We also applaud the no-doubt deliberate irony by the anonymous civil servant in the Department of Finance who named the ostensibly impoverished region after one of the world's leading luxury car brands.) But no one is going to play for, still less die for, the Border Midlands and West region, or any of the other unmemorable regional creations we have indulged in over the past decades. If we are serious about regional development, we have to identify regions that have economies of scale and with which we can identify.

The selection of a limited number of urban areas for development would help create critical mass. A recent example of how to approach this is the proposal for fourteen gateway centres on the island of Ireland.[1] In our view, these centres should not be designated on a 'top down' basis. Rather, centres should be invited to compete for designation, with selection based on pre-specified criteria, which, in addition to the normal economic ones, should include commitment to a high-quality environment, conservation of key natural and built features etc. The experience has been good with the competition to select the IT capital of Ireland (won by Ennis) and with the designation of areas for urban and village renewal – where local authorities and their associated business, environmental and community partners are invited to submit proposals according to specified criteria; these are subjected to independent review before a decision is taken. It is important to allow a high degree of autonomy and local engagement in the process of designing and implementing gateway centres. This allows scarce infrastructure investment to be allocated where the payoff to effort is likely to be greatest. Unless there is local commitment and support, such investment may prove fruitless. And we cannot know beforehand which areas have the energy, commitment and imagination to make the most of scarce investment support. As has happened in the US, some communities may choose not to develop further, or at least demur from being 'fast-tracked'. They should be allowed to grow slowly if such is their wish. Instead of a big bang, where fourteen centres are chosen and all the available infrastructure investment is spread between them, our idea is that action is taken incrementally, with those most active in providing parallel complementary support and making the most of investment as it happens gaining further support, and those who, for various reasons, are not so engaged or successful receiving less or none. In other words, we go with 'winners'.

# CHAPTER 8

# Accommodation

The madness that has been the Irish property market in the 1990s has abated. This pause gives us a chance to focus on some of the problems our recent rush to build has generated, and to make changes so we'll be ready for the next accommodation Klondike.

Wherever poets, Nobel laureates, artists, craftspeople, and sportsmen and sportswomen gather in Ireland, the conversation inevitably turns to the price of housing. Higher things give way to the mundane fascination with real-estate price movements. It's a topic in which we can all join; the property sections of the print and electronic media ensure that we are never short of a conversation piece. In the mid to late 1990s, even the most humble of shebeens rose in value, so that anyone anywhere with any property ownership could observe their riches grow. While this has been fed shamelessly at times by the enthusiasm of the press and their advertisers – Lord Rothmere commented that 'News is what someone somewhere doesn't want printed. The rest is advertising' – the phenomenon was real. There were dramatic rises in the real price of accommodation over the 1995 to 2000 period. These rises embraced house and apartment prices, and rents. These increases have borne especially heavily on recent recruits to the labour force, and this in turn is a source of pressure on wages, as workers attempted to recoup the increase in their living costs. The situation also increases the housing subsidy payable to those, in employment or otherwise, who are not able to afford to house themselves. Expenditure on rent supplementation under the social welfare allowance increased from €95.6 million in 1997 to €128.2 million in 1999, with an estimated 41,500 people in that year – one third of the renting population – in receipt of public assistance.[1]

But house prices fell in late 2001 in money terms by 2%–5%. When you add in the fact that general price inflation has been of the order of 4%–5%, this amounts to a near 10% price drop in real terms. This fall is all the more striking given that the number of housing starts in 2001 declined. If this fall had not taken place, the price fall would have been greater.

In the 1990s, in response to the rise in price over the 1993 to 2000 period, there was also a large increase in the supply of new accommodation, with the number of completions rising from 21,000 in 1993 to about 50,000 in 2000. The number of one-off houses built in the countryside has been increasing, rising to about 18,000 in the year 2000.[2]

There is a rising number of asylum seekers who must be housed by local or other public authorities, in part because they are not permitted to earn an income that would allow them to house themselves. There is continuing difficulty in housing Travellers.

The 'design content' in most new accommodation is low – very few architects are involved. There is very low energy efficiency in the older housing stock, leading to considerable fuel poverty for those on low incomes.

The predominant political concerns have been about the plight of the first-time buyer. This concern was reflected in the content of the Government-sponsored Bacon reports and subsequent policy action, notably incentives (special allocations) to local authorities to provide land with water and sewage services, increased budgets for social housing, the removal of tax incentives to provide rental accommodation, increased stamp duty on purchase of second homes.

Major political concerns about the needs of lower-income families led to the inclusion of the 'social housing land' provision in the

Planning Act, which requires that up to 20% of land for housing be made available at agricultural land value to the local authority for social housing.

Tax incentives have been provided in a rolling series of programmes for developments in urban areas perceived as being in decline, in towns and villages in a more focused way, in specified coastal resorts, and in the Upper Shannon region. Political and institutional responsibility has been dispersed, with the Department of Environment and local government having responsibility for the various urban programmes, and the Departments of Tourism and Finance respectively having responsibility for coastal resorts and the Upper Shannon. These incentives have endowed landowners in the benefiting areas with very large capital gains. As regards the town and urban incentives, these have broadly helped reverse the decline in the status of city and town living, and revived their economies.

## Some Key Issues

Shelter is a fundamental human need. For those who rent, providing this shelter in the current housing market can absorb up to 40% of disposable income for new entrants to the labour force. For those of us who buy, the house or apartment is the largest single investment that most of us will make. But how and where we live is also a statement of our status, our self-image, literally our place in the world. Because it encapsulates so much of our finance and our psyche, accommodation is an issue of enormous interest, significance for well-being, and variety.

Out of the near infinite array of issues that we could address here under the accommodation heading, we have chosen to focus on the one-off house, the accommodating of Travellers, and the plight of the renter. We have done so because policy in all three areas is dysfunctional, and could benefit from discussion, debate and change.

## The expansion of one-off housing in the countryside – why is it happening and does it matter?

There are several explanations for this phenomenon. The first and perhaps the most important is the very powerful financial incentive facing landowners and the one-off house developer/owner. On the demand side, with site costs averaging about €50,000 or more, and construction costs – depending on how much labour is supplied by the family doing the development – costing about €75,000, this means that a three-bedroom new house can be supplied for about €125,000. This compares with prices in the order of €180,000 upward for a new house purchased in a cluster development. So the one-off is substantially cheaper for the family developing. On the supply side, the landowner sells land with a value for agriculture of about €5,000 as a site for €50,000 (sometimes it is transferred free to a family member, but the value of the capital asset so transferred does not diminish) and so there is an average capital gain per site of €45,000, which translates to an annual capital gain (with 18,000 one-off houses developed) of €810 million. This dynamic of cheaper housing for buyers and large capital gains for landowners, mainly farmers, goes far to explain the popularity of the one-off.

A second reason why the one-off is so popular is cultural preference: many of us like living in relative isolation on the 'half acre'. A third force is snobbery: fear of the social-housing content on house development sites. A fourth factor is limited awareness or concern about visual effects and potential damage to tourism. Many rural dwellers see landscape as being improved by one-off housing, but others, often inhabitants of cities and towns, see only despoliation.

But, unfortunately, the single house is not really the solution to the housing 'problem' for the following reasons:

> ➤ Extra infrastructure costs are not included in the cost to the purchaser/developer. Relative to cluster development, the

costs per unit of accommodation provided to improve the roads, supply and maintain water, sewage disposal, and electricity are high. There are no rates payable on domestic dwellings, so these extra costs are passed on to the general taxpayer, damaging the overall economy.

➢ There can be extra pressure on groundwater supplies. Most one-off houses use septic tanks to dispose of waste. These require good location, design, construction and regular maintenance, and if any of these is not provided, there is a serious risk of contamination. This, in turn, undermines national environmental policy, which in turn can lead to European Union action in the courts, which in turn damages

## PROTECTING GROUNDWATER IN SINGLE-HOUSE DEVELOPMENT

'There can be no doubt that groundwater and wells have been contaminated by effluent from conventional septic tank systems. In fact, septic tank systems are one of the main sources of bacteriological pollution of private wells. When choosing the location and type of an on-site system, developers should have regard to groundwater, its underlying vulnerability and any nearby source. Site vulnerability is placed in one of a number of categories – extreme, high, moderate, and low – and this is combined with a categorisation of the water resource into regionally important, locally important, or poor. These are combined in a two-dimensional matrix to yield a prescription for waste-water systems, ranging from 'Acceptable subject to normal good practice' to 'Not generally acceptable' unless a treatment system other than a conventional septic tank is installed and numerous other conditions are met. The conventional septic tank system is preferred where the subsoils are sufficiently permeable to prevent ponding at the surface but not so permeable that the effluent enters groundwater relatively untreated. Also, the subsoils need to be of sufficient thickness so that the effluent does not enter the bedrock too quickly with inadequate purification.'

Donal Daly, 'Effluent from On-Site Wastewater Treatment Systems for Single Houses: a potential hazard for Groundwater', *The GSI Groundwater Newsletter*, No. 39, 31 October 2001. See also http//www.epa.ie.

our European environmental reputation and our reputation as 'good Europeans'.

➤ There are landscape and tourism effects. Much one-off housing is of a scale and style that is judged by many not to be in harmony with the landscape in which it sits. This damage to the quality and character of landscape is difficult, but not impossible, to quantify. The costs of such damage are not borne by the householder. Rather, they are borne by those residents in the community and visitors from elsewhere in Ireland and overseas for whom the developments represent a visual loss. To the extent that these latter reduce their visits to and expenditure in the community in question, locals who depend on the tourism industry will be damaged.

➤ There is extra pressure on social services. It is at the heart of policy towards older people that they be encouraged and facilitated to stay at home as long as possible, to avoid institutionalisation in nursing homes and hospitals until this is necessitated by their medical condition. Ideally this is facilitated by ready access to shops, social interaction, visits by home help and other services. All of this becomes much more difficult and expensive if such people are living alone in isolated houses, where even 'meals on wheels' becomes a logistical challenge. There is an embryonic move to link older people living alone electronically so that they can avail of the internet and e-mail. Servicing this digitalisation is also made more expensive and logistically complex by one-off living. At the other end of the demographic spectrum, the needs of children for schooling and social interaction can be made more difficult.

➤ Extra pressure on transport infrastructure and increased car dependence. Few if any residents of one-off housing can avail of reliable public or collective private transport because the costs of providing such service would be exorbitant. And so residents must have a car or motorcycle, or remain relatively isolated.

## The discrimination against renters – why does it happen, and does it matter?

It is a peculiarity of Irish political life that the first-time buyer seems to command far more political 'clout' than renters. And this bias is reflected in the brief given to the authors of the Bacon Reports, and the ensuing recommendations and policy action, where in effect renters are discriminated against in favour of the first-time buyer. It is as if renters do not vote, or are so apolitical that they do not understand where their interest lies. Or perhaps they all view renting as a purgatory from which they will in due time emerge to the heavenly status of owners.

The discrimination has come in a variety of forms: the supply of investments in rental property has been reduced as a result of tax changes, removal of Section 23 incentives for non-owner occupiers in designated areas, and the removal of mortgage-interest relief for investors.[3] For an investor to buy a house and rent it out is regarded as much less socially desirable than for a first-time buyer to purchase it. The first-time buyer gets exemption from stamp duty and gets a grant. The investor in rental property gets neither. Local authorities will give priority to the provision of first-time buyer housing in their decisions about selling land serviced for development.

With growing incomes and population chasing a reducing supply of accommodation for rent, the inevitable consequence has been rising rents, often rising in real terms by 10%–25% per annum.

Renters below certain income thresholds do benefit from rent subsidies, and some portion of rental payment is tax deductible, and this allows people of low income who would otherwise be excluded from accommodation to rent.

Fortunately, some of the discrimination against renters has been removed in the budget for 2002, with the provision that investors can set mortgage-interest payments against rental income for tax purposes. Also, the higher stamp duty payable by investors has been reduced to the same rates payable by owner-occupiers. While this is very welcome, it is notable that it has been justified not on the basis of fairness to renters or wider economic efficiency, but as a boost to the flagging construction sector.

## The Travellers

Thousands of years from now, archaeologists and anthropologists disinterring the remains of Ireland's twenty-first-century suburbs will marvel at, and be puzzled by, the encirclement of all open spaces by great boulders. They will conclude perhaps that mysterious religious rites took place there of unknown character. And, in a way, they will be right. The new religion, which generates as much passion as ever did the arrival of St Patrick, and which unifies communities in ways that religions can only dream of, is KEEP THE TRAVELLERS OUT. Why the passion and the ensuing innovations in boulder movement and placing?

The reasons seem to be threefold:

➢ The first is fear of property-value depreciation. A Traveller settlement is perceived to reduce the value of adjacent property (although there is no systematic evidence for this). The higher property values go the greater the potential loss: a 10% reduction in value on a €50,000 house is less than the same percentage reduction in the value of a €400,000 house.

➢ The second is worry about increased litter and general unsightliness, lack of sanitation, poor hygiene, and increased violence, begging and petty crime. Of these, perhaps litter is the greatest immediate issue. There is considerable variation in the extent to which litter is, in fact, a problem. On some sites it is obvious and pervasive, while on other Traveller sites there is virtually none.

➢ The third is social snobbery and racism, the view that Travellers are in some sense culturally and socially inferior, and therefore living adjacent to them is damaging. It is interesting to note that, based on a survey of 1500 households completed in 2001 by the Urban Institute, Travellers are less popular than any of the main immigrant groups.

**Table 5**

**Personal Attitude to Minority Groups**

|  | Irish Travellers | Chinese | Black African/ Caribbean | Eastern Europeans |
|---|---|---|---|---|
|  | % | % | % | % |
| Very Positive | 8 | 8 | 7 | 8 |
| Positive | 45 | 57 | 44 | 47 |
| Negative | 28 | 11 | 18 | 16 |
| Very Negative | 9 | 4 | 7 | 6 |
| Don't Know | 11 | 20 | 24 | 23 |

For a number of reasons, it is important that Ireland address the Traveller accommodation issue. Traveller infant mortality is high, and formal education levels, life expectancy and so on are low relative to the settled community – and this is related to inadequacy in accommodation. There is a case in social justice terms for intervening so as to give a child born into a Traveller family a better life chance than most receive at present. But there are also strong economic arguments. Minority cultures that are marginalised, i.e. that do not enter the economic and social mainstream, are especially vulnerable to drug and alcohol addiction, and other forms of social disintegration. And once such addictions take hold, they are difficult to reverse. If crime and anti-social behaviour become rooted, the challenge this poses to Traveller parents and their children becomes ever more difficult to overcome. And the costs to the rest of society also rise exponentially.

## Lessons for the Future

The dramatic rises in house prices and building costs, which have been characteristic in Ireland for the past five years or more, stretched all delivery mechanisms (builders, suppliers, local authority management, engineering and planning services, policy development and delivery) to the extent that there was no time and sometimes little interest in looking beyond the immediate to the quality of what was being achieved, to the economic implications in terms of the burdens imposed on future generations, the social costs and the environmental performance.

What's good for the individual builder is not always good for the industry. It is fashionable for developers to decry the delays in the planning system that slow down the pace of development. Appeals by organisations such as An Taisce are a particular target. In 2000 and 2001 there were many complaints concerning the uncertainty engendered by provisions in the Planning Act requiring up to 20% of the land in any development be made available for social housing. The combination of delay and uncertainty has undoubtedly reduced the prospects for individual developers. However, by slowing down the expansion in supply, these factors have also had the effect of maintaining house prices – the more accommodation supplied, other things being equal, the lower the price. Without the much decried social housing provisions which restricted supply, we could well have observed a collapse in the price of new houses in 2001 and thereafter. The industry should light a candle to Minister for Environment Noel Dempsey and raise their collective glasses in a toast to An Taisce for restricting supply and holding up prices.

The decline in house prices, and the slow-down in both demand and supply of accommodation provides an opportunity to take stock, and redirect policy and performance in ways that are more sustainable economically, socially and environmentally.

## Strong Incentives for High-Quality Cluster Development

The one-off housing boom has played an important role in meeting a large and growing proportion of accommodation needs at reasonable private costs to purchasers, and has provided substantial capital gains to landowners – in the order of over €800 million annually[4] – but at costs to the wider society in terms of provision of more costly infrastructure, increased travel times and associated energy use and greenhouse gas and pollution emissions, potential negative impacts on landscape and tourism, increased risk of contamination of groundwater, and rising social costs as residents become older and less able. The benefits are largely in the present, while the costs will be borne in the future.

The incentives facing landowners and prospective house purchasers have overwhelmingly favoured and encouraged the one-off house. Until these advantages are changed, the present will continue to be favoured, and the future will bear the cost. The solution is to change the incentives, so that cluster development is favoured.

But not everywhere. There are parts of Ireland that are losing population, and that have no town nodes to act as a demographic counter-weight.[5] In such areas, there is a case for facilitating and encouraging accommodation in the countryside that at least maintains the existing accommodation stock. Such encouragement should focus, in the first instance, on the refurbishment and further development of the existing housing stock. In these areas, tourism is likely to be the main sector with growth potential, so the need to maintain landscape and design standards is especially compelling.

Cluster development can be achieved in a variety of ways. The overarching idea is captured by the philosophy of the Greek General Xenophon: 'I should like the enemy to think that it is easy for him in every direction to retreat.' Make it as easy as possible to retreat from the one-off except where rural depletion is manifest.

For cluster development, land in a suitable location could be purchased by local authorities, serviced with appropriate infrastructure, and the land sold off to individuals and developers at a cost that was

**ENERGY EFFICIENCY IN HOUSING**

'Thirty-two new "passive" houses in Kronsberg, a suburb of Hanover, Germany, use 10%–20% of the energy of conventional houses. Walls are thick, with up to 16 inches of insulation, doors seal tightly, and windows are triple glazed. The incoming air does not mix with the outgoing air, but by passing alongside it through a series of chambers in a heat exchanger, it absorbs 80% of the outgoing air's heat. Thus, without the aid of any heating element, air that enters at a freezing temperature is brought all the way to 68°F before it begins circulating through the house, by the air that's being expelled at 72°F. The incoming air goes first to the kitchen and the bathrooms, where it picks up heat from appliances and people, then flows to cooler areas like bedrooms before leaving the house at 72°F. Only when the external temperature falls below 23°F is a backup heater needed. Solar collectors on the roof heat the water, while high-efficiency appliances and compact fluorescent lamps cut electricity use in half. A 1,400 foot three-bedroom duplex goes for $180,000, about 5% more than a comparable dwelling built to a lower energy efficiency standard.'

Henry Muller, 'Winds of Change', *Fortune*, Europe Edition, No. 6, March 26 2001, pp. 30–40

lower than the prices they would have to pay for one-off sites. The transfer price is crucial; it must be equal to or lower than the value of one-off sites. Tax incentives could be provided to encourage cluster development in locations pre-designated by the planning authorities.

One-off developments outside the areas losing population noted above should be charged the costs of providing infrastructure. This would simultaneously ensure that these costs were not passed on to the general taxpayer, and increase the incentive to avail of the sites provided in the cluster developments.

High design standards – relating to landscape protection, energy efficiency, protection of water quality and other environmental features, conservation of key features in buildings being re-furbished – should be required and enforced.

### Do not discriminate against renters

There is an economic argument for increasing the proportion of households that rent in Ireland, on the basis that it enhances flexibility and ability to move from job to job, and, specifically, to move out of Dublin and take jobs in other parts of Ireland without incurring all the transaction costs of selling and buying property. There is also a fairness argument, as renters are often those with limited or no ability to buy property. To this end, it is important that the discrimination against those providing rental accommodation, including ability to set off interest payments against income for tax purposes, has been corrected. These changes, undertaken when real property values seem to be in decline, will facilitate some real growth in the rental sector and a lowering of rents.

### Provide Travellers with incentives to solve their own accommodation needs, via the already existing channels for development approval

There seems to be no reason except access to capital why Travellers could not solve their own accommodation requirements. Grants could be made available to develop sites; it would be up to Travellers to form cooperatives to bid on developable land, and put together proposals for its development as sites.

However, this presents huge difficulties. Anyone who has ever tried to get a large group to agree on where to go for a walk or which film to watch knows that the costs of organising such a venture increase exponentially as the numbers involved rise.

This analysis is relevant to the Traveller case, because anecdotal evidence indicates that sites with a small number of Travellers tend to be well managed, tidy and not disruptive. As sites get larger, it becomes more difficult and costly to manage individual social activity and behaviour, and one family 'free riding', as regards litter for example, undermines the endeavour and standards of others, and the system breaks down. There are parallels here with the management of

## COLLECTIVE ACTION AND TRANSACTION COSTS

Whenever a group joins together voluntarily to achieve collective action, it has to address the challenge of transaction costs and free riders. 'Transaction costs' arise because of the time and effort it takes to make decisions and then implement them. These costs can become so high that they exceed the potential ensuing benefits. These transaction costs are important considerations when examining any proposals for collective action. It is also the case that, the larger the group, the more likely it is that there will be what economists call 'free riders', people who take the benefit from the collective action but try to escape any of the costs. This idea of individuals benefiting at the expense of the common good has been characterised as 'the tragedy of the commons'.[6] The argument goes as follows: if there is a commons to which everyone has free access for grazing animals, then it will inevitably be destroyed, because each individual has an incentive to keep adding stock, even though it is clear to all that the commons is being destroyed. And this happens because each individual knows that if he or she cuts back on use, their place will simply be taken by another. The psychology is that if the commons is going to be destroyed anyway, I'll get in there while there is still something to be got. This explains why a trawler owner in Killybegs does not reduce his fishing of cod even though the species is clearly being fished to destruction. He keeps at it as long as there are fish to be got, because forbearance on his part will achieve nothing; fishermen from elsewhere in Ireland or Europe will simply take his place. To make collective action work, the transaction costs have to be reduced sufficiently to the point where action that yields a net benefit is possible, and participants must have some incentive to join the club and not 'free ride' on the efforts of others. This entails enforcing sanctions on offenders.

public housing. Tony Fahey and colleagues at the Economic and Social Research Institute (ESRI) have noted in their survey of local-authority flat complexes that those that have clear and consistent management of access and facilities provide a much higher standard of social and physical environment than those that do not. They note the discrepancy between how private flat complexes are managed – with their limited access, levies to fund maintenance, management committees and structures – with their public-sector counterparts, where often none of the above are in place. And the same logic surely applies to Traveller sites.

If Travellers themselves were to take the initiative to come forward with development proposals, they would have to comply with and meet the standards provided for in development plans, and be subject to review by An Bord Pleanála. The need to come together with a coherent plan would likely limit proposals to relatively small groups, or, where larger scale proposals were proposed, having in place a coherent and effective management structure to overcome transactions costs and free-rider problems. Government could provide generous grant aid for site acquisition and development, and also provide some training and current funding to finance site management, including, especially, site access and maintenance. This 'bottom up' style of addressing the problem that integrates Traveller settlement into the normal routines of development is much more likely, in our view, to result in successful resolution of the problem than the present 'top down' approach. Government could also provide legal advice and financial support where legal challenges were gratuitously delaying progress.

Ownership of the sites would rest with the Traveller group, and there would be provision for division and privatisation under certain circumstances. How to handle the need for mobility? This would be a matter of arranging exchange or rental of space in other Traveller sites. A central reservation scheme could be used to facilitate the optimum 'fit' between the travelling desires of individual families and the availability of space. We are convinced that until Travellers have property rights in sites, and responsibility for their maintenance and management, difficulties will persist and intensify, with catastrophic consequences for the life prospects of Traveller children, and big losses also for the wider society.

# CHAPTER 9

# Traffic Congestion

*'Americans will put up with anything provided it doesn't block traffic.'* Dan Rather

One of the most obvious side-effects of the rapid growth of the Irish economy has been the substantial worsening of traffic congestion in urban areas. Increases in car ownership are strongly related to increases in household income. In addition, more disposable income tends to result in an increase in trip frequency. If we take car ownership as a proxy for congestion, it has been shown that of all the environmental impacts of the boom the increase in congestion has been the most strongly related to economic growth.[1]

Car ownership has grown by 7% per annum over the 1990s (Figure 16). The number of private vehicles has doubled since 1990. Ownership rates were 330 per 1,000 in 1998, compared with the figure of 342 per 1,000 predicted for 2011. Ireland's urban transport infrastructure was already poorly equipped to deal with the levels of traffic existing prior to the boom. The rapid increase in car ownership and congestion has made a bad situation worse as the growth in road space has not kept pace and improvements in public transport have been slow to materialise.

The rising level of car ownership has led to an increasing reliance on the private motor vehicle as the preferred mode of transport. Peak and off-peak trips more than doubled between 1991 and 1999. The expansion in vehicle numbers has considerable implications for

117

vehicular emissions and congestion in urban areas, particularly in Dublin where improvements in road networks, traffic management and public transport have not kept up with the rising demand for road space. Housing policy during the boom has been particularly inadequate and the spread of the Dublin commuter belt to include virtually all of Leinster and even further afield has led to many undesirable side-effects. These include a spread of congestion, increased travel time to work, rising frustration and stress, increased fuel use and associated greenhouse gases and other pollutants.

## The Costs of Urban Road Congestion[2]

There is a range of costs associated with road congestion:

> **Air Pollution**: Congested traffic means frequent acceleration, deceleration and idling engines. Emissions from cars can be up to 250% higher under congested conditions than under free-flowing traffic. $CO_2$ emissions contribute significantly to global warming and, in the Irish case, this is of particular concern given the current 'overshoot' of our limit set by the Kyoto Protocol. Other pollutants include $NO_X$, VOCs, CO and particulate matter, the latter two being particularly damaging to human health. Transport is the source of most fine and ultra-fine particles in the air we breathe, and these are now associated with lung and other health dysfunction. The majority of the local air pollution in our cities, and the associated health and other dysfunctions are a product of emissions from road-based transport.

> **Noise Pollution**: Increased numbers of vehicles contribute to the level of noise pollution in an area. According to a recent OECD report, high levels of transport noise can contribute to sleep loss, high blood pressure and cardiovascular disease. The report also notes that current EU limits on noise emission levels are much higher than levels consistent with health and comfort.

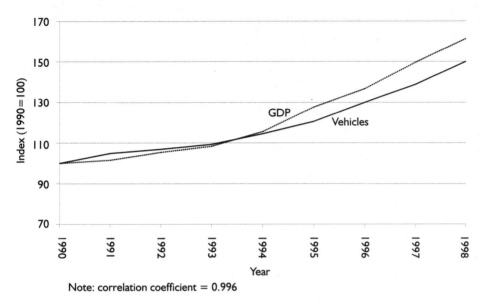

Note: correlation coefficient = 0.996

Figure 16: GROWTH IN GDP AND VEHICLE NUMBERS 1990–1998

➤ **Accidents**: The number of accidents and the relative cost of insurance is proportional to the level of traffic. In congested areas, while the number of accidents may increase, many are small 'bumps and scrapes' and do not involve injury. However, congested traffic is undoubtedly more stressful than free-flowing traffic and the frustration of being 'hemmed in' in traffic can lead to a desire by drivers to make the most of clear roads via faster driving, thereby increasing the link between congestion and accidents.

➤ **Road Wear and Tear**: Wear and tear is primarily thought to relate to heavy vehicles and weather factors, but studies show the impact of high levels of smaller, slow-moving private vehicles to be significant over time. The cost of this damage is not simply the cost of road repairs, but also the discomfort and damage to cyclists, and to other motorists and their vehicles from poor road surface integrity.

119

➢ **Energy Usage:** Twenty percent of world-wide energy use is for transport. Congestion reduces the efficiency (kilometres per litre) of fuel consumption and thus increases energy use per kilometre travelled.

➢ **Time Loss:** 'Time is money' and, in an economy with rising living standards, people place an ever-higher value on their time. Although there is much disagreement over the valuation of the time lost due to the lower average speed of congested traffic, it is clearly an undesirable aspect of travel in urban areas. Congested traffic contributes to levels of stress and anxiety and also increases the incidence of 'road rage'.

## Traffic Congestion in Dublin

Undoubtedly, the largest costs of the increase in the number of private vehicles on the road and increases in trip frequency arise in the Dublin region. Peak-time journeys into the Dublin region increased by 64% between 1991 and 1998 and the modal share accounted for by public transport actually fell by 8%. In addition, a survey conducted by Dublin Corporation of average vehicular speeds in peak-time traffic has shown inbound and outbound peak traffic to have slowed by 27.5% and 20% respectively between 1994 and 2000. How much is this additional congestion costing us? No single consistent estimate is available, as there is no agreement on the weighting and true cost of the negative effects described earlier and the valuation of these impacts is extremely difficult. However, estimates of the costs of congestion have been put at between 2% and 8% of GDP, with private cars accounting for some 58% of this cost. It is estimated by the Dublin Transportation Office that congestion costs in terms of lost time in the city amount to over €0.6 billion per annum.

Much of the activity in the new Dublin economy is deriving from developments along the 'C ring' motorway circling the city to the west, with nodes at Swords/Dublin airport (Motorola, Hertz),

Blanchardstown/Mullhuddart (IBM complex), West Dublin/North Kildare (Intel, Hewlett Packard), Tallaght (Citywest, Parkwest) and Leopardstown/Sandyford (Microsoft, Cherrywood Technology Park). This development of an 'edge city' is characteristic of developments in many urban areas, but has happened with particular rapidity in the Dublin region. Except for some apartment development in the inner city, most housing is low-density suburban, and this process of urban sprawl and dispersal seems to be accelerating, with much of the development leapfrogging the established commuter belt. Between 1997 and 1998, the level of planning permissions for new housing in the outer Leinster counties (60km+ from Dublin) grew by 40%, compared with a 14.7% growth in the Dublin region, and long-distance commuting by rail and bus, but mainly by car, is becoming characteristic. This has led to further congestion, increased travel time to work, rising frustrations and stress, increased fuel use and associated pollution.

## The Economist's Analysis of Road Congestion

The principal problem in relation to road space reflects quite closely the problems raised in Garrett Hardin's classic piece on the 'tragedy of the commons' (1968): once road tax is paid, everyone has access to the road network at all times (unless the road is tolled). In the short term, the supply of road space is relatively fixed and thus, beyond a certain point, marginal congestion costs increase. As more and more cars come onto the roads, the costs imposed by each additional car become greater and greater. If one car stays off the road, the other cars continuing to use it are rewarded by less congestion. Thus, there is a classic free-rider problem: Why should I stay off the roads and let others benefit? This is the standard problem in relation to common-property type resources. It explains why urging motorists to leave the car at home has a very limited effect. When there are large numbers of car owners such 'moral suasion' is unlikely to work.

So, what is the solution? The economist's analysis of the situation is that individuals must be made to face some proportion of the costs imposed on others by their journey. Note the concept of marginal cost is the key – that is to say, what they pay should relate to the costs of an additional journey rather than a fixed amount at the beginning of the year (such as road tax or insurance). Estimates have shown that private motorists pay in motor taxes an amount greater than total congestion costs. However, this is not the issue. These fixed charges do not address the problem of congestion – in fact, they could even encourage more frequent car use: Why leave a fully taxed and insured car sitting idle in the driveway? But making individuals pay some of the marginal costs imposed on others by each trip would lead to a more efficient use of road space. (Note, however, that strictly speaking, making motorists pay the full marginal cost is not necessarily optimal. This is because there may be some costs imposed upon society, for example, in terms of lost productivity/sales, by reducing the volume of cars coming into a city.)

In addition to these so-called 'demand-side' measures, which influence people's demand for road space, supply-side measures are important instruments to alleviate congestion. Such measures alter the supply of different forms of road space.

## Measures to Address Road Congestion: The Case of Dublin

There have been several new initiatives and developments with regard to traffic management in recent years. These can be categorised as supply-side and demand-side measures. While the focus here is on Dublin, the analysis can be applied to other Irish cities.

### Supply-side Measures

Dublin now has a state-of-the-art control centre that runs twenty-four hours a day, which facilitates rapid reaction to any incident that is hindering the flow of traffic. Sensors in the road convey information to the control centre, and a traffic-light control and monitoring system which adapts the traffic-light sequencing is in place. Electronic parking signs provide motorists with information on parking availability in the city's multi-storey car parks.

Dublin City Council has introduced new directives on the management of roadworks. However, anecdotal evidence would suggest that the public has yet to be convinced that this policy is working.

Extensive development of cycle lanes throughout the city is underway, and while the quality of the network is still somewhat patchy, the city appears to be working towards a better network. When completed, the total length of cycle lanes in Dublin will amount to 180km. These remain a relatively under-utilised resource.

A total of eleven 'quality bus corridors' (QBCs – dedicated bus lanes that operate from 7.00am to 7.00pm with traffic signal priorities) have been implemented. However, the continuation of cash fares has led to the bunching of buses on QBCs. On the most successful of the bus routes implemented to date, there has been a 190% increase in passenger levels during the morning peak. But there is concern regarding the distributional impacts of the QBC policy with a suggestion that service on the QBC routes has been kept up at the expense of other routes. Also, park-and-ride facilities are completely inadequate and result in considerable costs to those who live in areas close to QBCs who have to tolerate people parking on kerbs.

While it is easy to be critical of Dublin Bus, it is important to note that the subsidy it receives is very low in terms of European norms. In addition, it has faced difficulties in terms of industrial relations and the ability to hold on to drivers in today's tight labour market. This has certainly had a detrimental effect on the quality of services. However, increases in subsidy should be linked to increased efficiency in the management of the network and the introduction of integrated ticketing. Elements of competition should also be introduced, especially in the provision of services that Dublin Bus has been reluctant to undertake – for example, the granting of a license to the aircoach service resolved the problems of people being stranded in Bus Áras instead of being delivered to the city centre and suburban hotels.

## Future Developments on the Supply Side

Some very welcome developments are the start of construction of the Dublin Port Tunnel, which will divert heavy traffic away from Dublin city centre, the deregulation of the taxi markets, which helped to reduce queuing times, the proposal to open up public transport to competitive tender and the commencement of the construction of the Luas light-rail system. However, the park-and-ride facilities for LUAS are less than clear and, unless adequate provisions are put in place, those living within the vicinity of LUAS stations will be considerably inconvenienced.

The potential exists at present to provide commuters with a great deal of information to improve flow through the transport network and minimise waiting time via advanced commuter information systems. As wireless communication advances and wireless devices saturate the market, it is likely that a wide range of information from 'When is the next bus to town?' to 'Where can I find an on-street parking space?' will become available to commuters at the touch of a button. The increased efficiency and reliability that will come with this will certainly improve the attractiveness of public transport.

## Demand-side Measures

**Traffic Calming and Pedestrian Priority**: These measures are also supply-side measures but have a big impact on the private motorist and so we have included them as demand-side. There has been a great deal of development in terms of traffic calming and pedestrian prioritisation recently in Dublin. Speed ramps have been installed throughout the suburbs in an effort to slow through-traffic and thereby increase safety. There has also been work in the city centre to restrict through-traffic by the use of 'traffic cells'. The concept of a traffic cell is that traffic may move freely within a given area, however there are restrictions on moving between areas for private transport. Thus there is a limit placed on routes that a private vehicle may take to get to another traffic cell. The objective of this project is to reduce 'through-traffic' in the city as a whole.

Much work has also been put into making the city more pedestrian-friendly. Measures taken include: the installation of more pedestrian crossing facilities, increasing 'green man' time, redesign of junctions with pedestrian safety in mind, and timers that count down to the next crossing to improve pedestrian patience. However, these improvements in the provisions for pedestrians come at the expense of traffic flow.

**Parking Policy**: This is one of the most potent tools at the disposal of Dublin City Council for influencing modal choice and is also a significant source of revenue. The pricing of parking can be used to charge the private motorist for the marginal costs imposed by their travel. The power of this tool depends on the proportion of spaces under the control of the policymaker. The success of this tool will be greatly enhanced if private non-residential (PNR) spaces are covered by the policy. This is not the case at present.

Dublin City Council has been following a steady programme for 'rolling back' the free spaces in the city and bringing all free on-street parking under control by the use of parking restrictions and paid parking. All revenues are ring-fenced for traffic management measures.

This system owes a considerable portion of its success to a thorough enforcement policy as, without the risk of penalty, parking as a policy tool would be much less effective. Wheel clamping and tow-away services were introduced in the Dublin area in 1998, and have resulted in a 60% decrease in illegal parking. In addition, in multi-storey car parks in Dublin, it is a legal requirement that the hourly cost of parking increase with the length of stay.

**Fiscal Measures**: These include excise duty on motor fuels, sales tax on vehicles (VRT), annual road tax and tax on commuting expenses. The sales tax rate and the annual road tax on private vehicles depend on engine size. These were introduced as luxury taxes rather than for environmental purposes and do not take into account engine characteristics such as emissions and noise. However, there are incentives for purchasers of hybrid (battery and petrol) motor vehicles although such cars are still relatively expensive. In urban areas the size of the vehicle is probably more important as an indicator of social costs than engine capacity. The exponential growth of large 'all terrain vehicles' is generating an increasingly severe problem on the narrow streets of the city. The tax rate ought to take account of a vehicle's dimensions in order to discourage the wasteful use of scarce urban road space. Another abuse is the evasion of higher taxes on these vehicles by their classification under commercial as distinct from domestic use, with the paradoxical effect that a large van-like vehicle may have a lower road tax than a modest saloon car.

## Future Developments on the Demand Side

A report commissioned by the Government in 1998 recommended a road-pricing charge of €3.81 per car entering Dublin city centre during peak hours, and estimated that the system would pay for itself within a year. However, these recommendations have not been adopted and there is no congestion charging at present. The best example of an implemented road-pricing scheme comes from Singapore (see box p.128), but it must be noted that Singapore has an exemplary public transport system that includes a metro. Dublin does not and, therefore, the price sensitivity for private motoring is likely to be substantially lower. Road pricing does not seem to be a tool that is favoured by Irish policy makers. The principal objections to it include the cost of the technology, the civil rights implications of electronic tagging and political unacceptability.

Parking pricing has a number of potential advantages over road pricing. Perhaps, most importantly, it is an established pricing infrastructure, and is an accepted charge as people can see what they are buying, i.e. time in the space. In addition, parking pricing can do more than simply trigger a modal shift in order to influence congestion levels and emissions. If parking is priced so as to ensure a certain average level of occupancy in a given area, it can also have a positive impact on traffic flow and congestion. If parking is incorrectly priced and spaces are allowed to reach complete saturation, parking is itself indirectly responsible for additional traffic congestion as vehicles cruise while searching for a space. However, parking policy also has its own limitations and concerns. As a means of affecting traffic within a city, parking-pricing policy will have no effect upon 'through traffic' (vehicles that are not looking to park) and may even encourage this type of traffic if it impacts positively on overall congestion levels. Those whom the authorities wish to see using the parking facilities – the shoppers – are more price-sensitive than commuters. Thus, the more the price is raised, the greater the proportion of commuters who will park.

## Lessons for the Future

Of all the environmental pressures facing Ireland, congestion is the most highly correlated with GDP growth and has risen most rapidly during the boom. Therefore, a slowing of the growth rate of the economy and an associated reduction in the rate of increase of car ownership would be good news in terms of cooling the worsening situation with regard to traffic congestion in urban areas. But it would be defeatist to suggest that we should welcome a recession because we cannot deal with our traffic problems during a boom. In fact, it is important to acknowledge that economic growth increases the resources at our disposal for tackling problems such as congestion and pollution, while during a recession it is all too likely that these problems will be ignored. Traffic congestion was a problem even before the boom and addressing the problem remains a key challenge in managing the transition to sustainable growth. Poor transport infrastructure and the impact of congestion on the quality of life of urban and suburban residents are key impediments to the growth of the economy. It is most important that the Government follow through on the investment in transport infrastructure envisaged in

## ELECTRONIC ROAD PRICING (ERP) IN SINGAPORE

Singapore pioneered road pricing. The city state has millions of cars wanting to use its very scarce road space. Without intervention, gridlock loomed. Part of the solution has been to charge for the use of road space, with the charges set at such a level that use of the road is reduced to the point where serious congestion does not arise. The charge varies according to the road that is being used, the time of day, and the day of the week. If the charges are too low to discourage congestion, then they are raised. If they are too high, such that the road space is being underused, then they are lowered. Revenues are used to manage the system, and to reduce the annual vehicle registration tax. Every motorist has to buy a card, just like a phone card, and insert it into a special machine mounted on the dash of the car. Every time he or she goes under an electronic gantry, the appropriate number of units is deducted from the card. If there are insufficient units on the card, or if the motorist has no card at all, the plate number is photographed as the car goes under the gantry, and the motorist in question is fined.

The benefits to the motorist are obvious: whenever or wherever they choose to drive, they are sure of relatively free-flowing traffic with associated reduction in time wasted, stress, pollution emissions, etc. The costs are also obvious: charges that at peak times can be very substantial.

The road charging system to be implemented in London is a flat fee of Stg£5 per trip. This is more like a levy or tax on motorists to finance public transport than a charge for use of road space, as it does not vary by road, and is not raised and lowered to achieve free-flowing traffic. If serious reduction of congestion is the goal, then the Singapore solution has much to offer. Its acceptability is enhanced by the availability of an excellent metro system, which provides an inexpensive option for commuters and shoppers.

the National Development Plan. However, a further challenge is how to manage the demand side while we wait for improvements on the supply side to materalise.

Measures to control the demand side include annual road and sales taxes on vehicles. The major flaw in how such fiscal instruments are used in regard to private transport is that, due to the structure of taxes and charges, the marginal costs of motoring – that is to say the costs of another journey by car – are far too low relative to the fixed costs. By the time one has bought one's car, and paid the sales tax, road tax and insurance, the costs of driving it seem rather low. At present, it costs the motorist much the same – in cash terms – to drive in the depths of the country, where she or he imposes no congestion costs on others, as to drive in the middle of Dublin in rush hour, where congestion costs rise exponentially with the number of cars on the road.

Annual road tax and possibly also the sales tax on cars should be reduced but marginal costs for driving in congested areas should be increased dramatically. This approach has been recommended by the OECD in its review of Ireland's economic performance in 2001. While it is often claimed by policy makers that existing taxes on private motoring are environmental taxes, their primary purpose is actually revenue raising and, apart from the differential in excise duty between unleaded and leaded petrol, they are not designed with environmental issues in mind. It is well known that the engine size is a poor measure of the environmental impact of a vehicle. Therefore, annual vehicle tax and vehicle sales tax should be adjusted to reflect better the emissions, noise characteristics, and size of vehicles. This can be done relatively easily based on the detailed specifications provided by car manufacturers. Indeed, it is now mandatory that each model of car has a label showing its level of $CO_2$ emissions. A national guide on fuel consumption and carbon dioxide emissions for all new car models is available at all garage forecourts and showrooms. These are new requirements under an EU directive on consumer information on the environmental aspects of motoring. All emissions characteristics of new cars are published and it would be relatively easy to come up with a more sophisticated sales and road tax system which could then be communicated to the public by labelling at point of sale. However, again our policy makers continue to rely on the ineffective approach of publishing pamphlets encouraging consumers to

## SOME CONSIDERATIONS FOR OPTIMISING THE USE OF ROAD SPACE

➤ The provision of more filter arrows. Anecdotal evidence suggests that filters in the suburbs are being removed and not necessarily in order to facilitate pedestrian crossings.

➤ Optimising the time that flashing amber-arrow filters are on. There are examples in Dublin where these lights turn red even when the pedestrian light is also red.

➤ The possibility of introducing 'left-turn on red' along the lines of the American system where cars turning right (as they drive on the right) may go through red lights so long as they stop first and then yield to traffic and pedestrians. 'Right on red' is, according to Woody Allen, California's sole contribution to American culture!

➤ Ensuring that all traffic lights have sensors. There are still plenty of traffic lights in the suburbs that do not seem to have sensors.

➤ The possibility of having movable lanes (a contra-flow system) on roads with 3 or more lanes e.g. in the USA and other countries, a 3-lane road would have 2 lanes inbound in the morning and 2 lanes outbound in the evening. However, the introduction of QBCs on most of the larger roads may mean that this is now a non-starter.

➤ Whether having bus lanes operate on a Saturday is appropriate. Is the traffic flow so much heavier on a Saturday in comparison with a Sunday that the lanes are necessary? Certainly, traffic seems to flow better on a Sunday – is this due to lower volume or more road space?

➤ Bus lanes should be colour-coded according to the times they operate.

➤ Whether bus lanes should also be car-pooling lanes, i.e. whether cars with three or more people should be permitted to use bus lanes? This would certainly facilitate those who live in areas with a poor bus service.

➤ Whether bus lanes that operate on a 24-hour basis make any sense given that buses (apart from a few private coaches) do not operate on a 24-hour basis?

> On the bridges and on some of the best roads around Dublin traffic often grinds to a halt due to the necessity of each driver placing coins or tokens in baskets at the toll booth rather than using a 'smart card' with dedicated lanes for such. We are sure this will eventually be dealt with as the problem is already obvious.

> Until smart cards are introduced, the possibility should be investigated of including a legal requirement that, once traffic flow in the vicinity of a toll plaza slows to a certain speed, the barriers must be left open.

> The exact rationale for tolls must be made clear, i.e. are they to raise revenue or are they to ration road space? Depending on the rationale, the placing of toll plazas may be arranged quite differently.

> Improving signposting would improve the flow of traffic. The signposting in Dublin is very poor. It is extremely difficult to see street signs on the sides of buildings, and looking for them while driving is very dangerous. In many cases there are no signs where the old sign has fallen off or been removed or a new building been erected. In any case, this form of signposting is of little use to motorists and cross-street signposting should be provided on all intersections.

> Performance data on changes in traffic flow as a result of the initiatives of the relevant authorities should be published online.

'do the right thing' rather than actually modifying policy instruments to reward those who do.

Even if significant changes are made, tax rates alone are unlikely to stem the rapid growth in car ownership and trip frequencies. The rise in oil prices in 2001 did little to reduce demand for petrol, suggesting that commuters are relatively insensitive to the price. Thus, energy taxes may have little impact. It seems as if road pricing is unlikely to be introduced, but second-best approaches such as more comprehensive parking charges and taxing parking as a benefit in kind have potential. However, preliminary results from work currently under way in UCD support the view that price sensitivity tends to be very low in transport in the absence of high-quality substitutes. Better public transport is thus a key factor in encouraging more efficient use of the car in urban areas.

While there is large investment under way to improve Dublin's public transport and to improve the flow of traffic via new road space, these are long-term projects. The provision of an integrated and efficient transport network for Dublin will certainly be enhanced by the proposal for a 'super authority' for Dublin's transport. This new authority for the Greater Dublin area will, amongst other things, prepare land use, transport strategies and implementation plans, and promote an integrated public transport system. This unified body will have all authority for decisions and, if properly constructed, will be very beneficial.

The national Climate Change Strategy hopes that reductions in energy use in the transport sector will reduce our overshoot of the Kyoto greenhouse gas limit by about 20%. This would come about through increased use of public transport, increases in excise duty on fuels, and greater fuel efficiency of vehicles. We will be assisted by the voluntary agreement between the EU and European, Japanese and Korean car manufacturers to reduce $CO_2$ emissions from new cars by an average of 25%. However, the bottom line is that, if the supply-side measures are not forthcoming, demand-side measures are likely to have little effect. This will reduce such measures to mere revenue raising without a significant reduction in congestion.

The short-term supply-side approach seems to be to make life difficult for the private motorist and thereby choke off demand. While those living on QBCs or the DART (despite the capacity limitations on the these modes) have an alternative to commuting by car, many parts of the city are very badly served by public transport. Thus, the policy of penalising the car owner imposes costs on those who have no alternative but to use private transport. In the short term, until the alternatives are in place, it is important to ensure that we do our utmost to provide incentives to push those who are able but unwilling into using public transport (presuming capacity is sufficient on, for example, the QBCs and DART) but also we must recognise that many commuters will still need to drive. Therefore, road space must be allocated as efficiently as possible for the competing modes of transport. Sight should not be lost of the need to ensure that all modes of transport are used most efficiently. Some of the issues that arise are presented in the box on pp.130-1. This has a Dublin focus but the issues are similar in other areas. More effort needs to be put into explaining the rationale for specific modifications to traffic flow, and performance data should be provided to show the improvement. This will be essential to convince the public that the short-term measures are in their interests.

# CHAPTER 10

# Environment

The environment can be defined as that part of our experience that we share – the air we breathe, the oceans we sail and fish in, the ozone layer, the greenhouse gases that maintain the planet's temperature and allow life to exist, the beauty of nature and our built surroundings.

A high quality of environment is both an important dimension of quality of life and a key requirement for economic performance. In Ireland, the well-being of our economy is intimately related to how well we manage our environment. Our tourism industry depends crucially on the reality and perception of a high-quality environment. No city, town or village that is serious about being a player in tourism can afford to destroy or damage its heritage and built endowments. No rural community wishing to maintain a steady flow of visitors can afford to destroy its landscape qualities. The food industry at the upper end of international markets depends on Ireland's 'green image' for its competitive advantage. Perhaps more fundamentally, no society wishing to attract the best and the brightest intellectual talents from around the globe – and to keep those talented people who grow up in it – can afford to diminish environmental quality. There is no instance of a 'silicon valley' type business and intellectual ferment locating in a degraded environment. When the world is your oyster, you don't set your compass for dross.

The problem from a policy point of view is that there is a time lag between debasing environmental endowments and incurring the costs. It may take a decade before the landscapes now under threat because of the explosion in one-off housing begin to damage tourism numbers and expenditure. Food can continue to be sold abroad on the basis of a pristine originating environment for up to ten years after the reality is otherwise. But the truth will out eventually. The practice of 'gombeenism', of ruthless exploitation of others, maximising short-term gain at the expense of the future, has dire consequences.

As we will see, there is evidence of 'environmental gombeenism' in much of our recent environmental performance. Part of the explanation lies in the rapid rate of recent change, which provides some justification for our inadequacies. For generation after generation, the Irish economy cantered along like a horse-drawn coach, moving slowly, encountering an occasional bump or pothole or highway robber along the way. The pace was leisurely, and the imprint on nature modest. Without warning, our coachmen found themselves transferred from the coach to the economic equivalent of the Shinkansen (bullet train) from Tokyo to Osaka, moving at heretofore unimaginable speed, and with no knowledge of the controls. Indeed, the one control they understood – the use of the interest rate to modulate investment volume – they found had been removed. It is little wonder that they had no time and little inclination or capacity to assess carefully the impact of their journey on the countryside, or to ensure that such impacts were benign.

The post Twin Towers world is an interesting time to examine Ireland's environmental performance for two reasons: the first is that many environmental challenges are linked positively or negatively to economic growth, and now that the growth train has slowed down, we can take the time to learn from our recent past. The second is that the Twin Towers experience highlights how interdependent the world is and how changes on one part of a system can impact on others. This provides a framework for examining environment within the wider framework of inter-linkages.

Ecology is the science of linkage, the intellectual framework for understanding interdependencies in nature, including the human imprint thereon. On 6 August 1945 US President Harry Truman spoke as follows: 'Sixteen hours ago, an American airplane dropped one bomb on Hiroshima, an important Japanese army base. That bomb had more power than 20,000 tonnes of TNT. It is an atomic bomb.' Thus was Prometheus unleashed; this event symbolises better than most the growing power of humans over nature, a power that has since grown a thousandfold. In a post-Twin Towers world, we revisit with apprehension the various parts of the world where the nuclear genie is truly out of the bottle. To the potential for nuclear cataclysm has been added the incremental damage we as a species inflict on various life forms and life-support systems of our planet, including depletion of the ozone layer, impacts on climate change, depletion of tropical forests and species, and now the more mundane, but no less frightening, challenge of biological contamination.

'Everything is connected to everything else in the universe.' So spoke the great American naturalist John Muir, and his words capture the essence of the environmental challenge. As we invent new products, new systems, new sources of energy, we must always understand that the effects of these products and these actions can extend far beyond what was originally envisaged. For example, when CFCs were invented, they provided the critical breakthrough that allowed inexpensive refrigeration, air conditioning and aerosol sprays to become pervasive. They are stable, non-toxic, and have no smell, so there was no reason at the time of their development to imagine that there could be any problem. Only later did the 'law of unintended consequences' come into play, as it became clear that chlorofluorocarbons were destroying the ozone layer in the atmosphere, which plays a crucial role in protecting us from the malign effects of ultraviolet light. There is also a link between environment, energy and social well-being, as exemplified by the links between fuel poverty, greenhouse gas and other emissions, and inadequacies in how low-income houses are insulated.

How we act as custodians of the endowment of nature and past generations has become regarded as a test of our ability as a species to manage our behaviour in the planet such that we don't, either by design or (more likely) by accident, leave future generations worse off than we are. There are various attempts to encapsulate our performance in a single indicator linked to GDP, and these are paralleled by more modest efforts to provide various indicators of environmental performance. The main use of such indicators is to track performance over time, usually either of emissions or of ambient quality, and see whether it is improving or otherwise. Such trends can also be linked to global, EU or national standards, to see whether and to what extent the desired standard is being met. In looking at Ireland's environmental performance, we find that in some domains it is impressively positive, while in others it is poor.

## FUEL POVERTY AND ENERGY CONSERVATION

'Poor people in Ireland spend about 13% of their income on energy. But in spite of spending this, many are still cold and damp in winter. These people also tend to buy bulkier, dirtier fuel like coal and slack, they burn it inefficiently in open fires, and they live in older, poorly insulated houses. Because of fuel poverty, lower-income people suffer disproportionately from respiratory diseases, and many older people die earlier than they should. The poor insulation means that much of the energy literally goes up the chimney, and this results in increased emissions of greenhouse gases and pollution. It has been estimated that a programme to achieve modern standards of energy conservation in all Irish housing would pay for itself in six years, it would improve our environmental performance significantly, and most important of all, it would give comfort and good health to thousands of our most vulnerable citizens.'

J. Peter Clinch and John Healy, 'Alleviating Fuel Poverty in Ireland: a Program for the 21st Century,' *International Journal for Housing Science*, vol. 23, no. 4, 1999, pp. 203–215. Vivienne Brophy, J. Peter Clinch, Frank J. Convery, John D. Healy, Ciarán King and J. Owen Lewis, *Homes for the 21st Century: The Costs and Benefits of Comfortable Housing in Ireland*, Energy Research Group and Environmental Institute, University College Dublin and Energy Action, Dublin, 1999

## Ireland's Performance[1]

### Improvements

**Dublin's smoke:** In the late 1970s and 1980s, the city's winters were inter-spersed with smoke pollution incidents that caused severe health and other problems, including premature death.[2] If this phenomenon had continued, it would have imposed serious costs on the city, not simply in terms of health and quality of life, but also in terms of image and attractiveness as a modern European city open for business at the cutting edge of financial and IT services. But a combination of normal economic forces led many to switch from (dirty) bituminous coal to clean natural gas, and a ban on the marketing, sale and distri-bution of bituminous coal did the rest. As regards smoke, Dublin's air quality is now up to the best European standards.

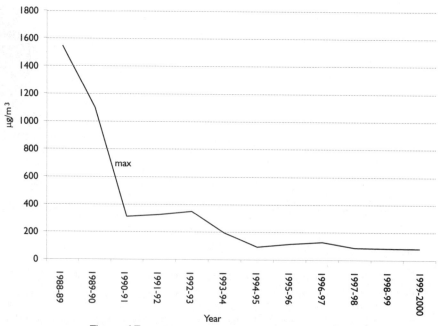

Figure 17: MAXIMUM DAILY SMOKE EMISSIONS IN DUBLIN

**Silage toxicity**: In the past, when silage (fermented grass) was being stored, it produced a liquor which, if it ran into water, would eliminate the oxygen in the receiving waters, resulting in dramatic fish kills. The ubiquitous fish kills associated with release of this highly toxic liquor by-product of silage production are a thing of the past, as a result of an information campaign and grants for storage.

**Industry**: A recent study has shown that across almost all environmental indicator variables (exceptions being the acidifying gases – sulphur dioxide, nitrogen oxide, carbon monoxide), those companies brought under the Integrated Pollution Control Licensing system have reduced emissions, some very substantially.[3]

## Deterioration or No Improvement

**Air quality indicators:** Unless a person relocates, they have no choice about the type of air they breathe. And air quality affects our well-being in numerous ways. Smoke is damaging to health. Acidity – caused by acid 'precursors' such as sulphur and nitrogen oxides – in the air damages buildings and plant life. High concentrations of carbon monoxide can be lethal. Over the period 1990 to 1998, some air emissions ($NO_x$, VOC, $N_2O$) increased by between 6% and 14%. Sulphur dioxide ($SO_2$) remained constant. This compares with GDP growth over the same period of 61%, so that, while deterioration in an absolute sense is evident in some quarters, the rate of deterioration is much lower than the rate of GDP growth.

**Housing and transport:** While incomes have risen, urban dwellers face increased road congestion, longer commuting distances, housing shortages, increased noise etc. Using house prices as a proxy for housing shortages and vehicle numbers as a proxy for congestion, it can be seen from Figure 18 that, unlike emissions to air, these environmental impacts have kept pace with GDP growth. While between 1990 and 1998, GDP increased by 61% and the volume of industrial production more than doubled, vehicle numbers increased by 50%

139

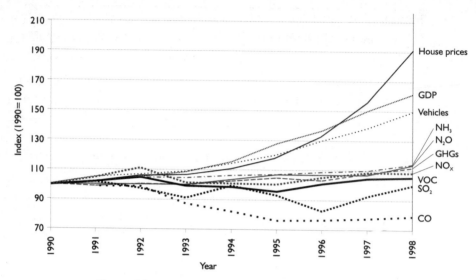

**Figure 18:** INDEXES OF GDP, VEHICLE NUMBERS AND SELECTED
AIR EMISSIONS, 1990–1998

and house prices doubled. The real rise in house prices has, of course, given existing (pre-boom) owners a substantial capital gain, but for new entrants at the margin, the incremental costs are substantial. Noise complaints to Dublin Corporation almost doubled between 1996 and 1998. The incidence of levels of particles (mostly from vehicle emissions) in some areas of Dublin is roughly twice recommended levels. These are particularly harmful when inhaled.

**Water quality**: By European standards, an unusually high proportion of our river system is classified as 'unpolluted', at 66.9%. However, the trend is negative as all categories of pollution, except the percentage 'highly polluted', have been increasing.

The unwillingness to meter and then charge households for water means that local authorities will be faced with either receiving a continuing subsidy from central government to finance the operation of the very expensive water supply and (especially) wastewater treatment plants that have been installed, or charging commercial and industrial users more than it costs to supply them so as to cross-subsidise the household sector.

**Table 6**

**Quality Status of Freshwater Rivers in Ireland, 1987–97, % of Total**

|                   | 1987-90 | 1995-97 |
|-------------------|---------|---------|
| Unpolluted        | 77.3    | 66.9    |
| Slightly Polluted | 12      | 18.2    |
| Moderately        | 9.7     | 14      |
| Heavily Polluted  | 0.9     | 0.9     |

Source: EPA

**Waste**: There has been rapid growth in waste generation over the past five years. Virtually all categories of waste have grown. Although some of this growth merely reflects better reporting, the Environmental Protection Agency (EPA) has noted that 'Where historical data is considered to be reasonably reliable, waste quantities appear to be increasing more or less in line with economic growth.'[4] Some specific findings:

> ➤ Municipal (households and commercial) account for only 13.4% of the total (excluding agriculture) in 1998, and 5% of the growth over the 1995–98 period.

> ➤ The recovery rate (re-use and recycling) overall is 26.6%, with the leading recovery sectors being end-of-life vehicles (96.0%), hazardous wastes (54.4%), manufacturing industry (51.4%), and construction waste (43.3%).

> ➤ The chemical industry dominates the generation of hazardous wastes, accounting for 89% of emissions arising in 1998.

> ➤ Of the best estimate of 296 thousand tonnes of hazardous waste arising, which includes non-industrial waste, 74 thousand tonnes, or 25% of the total, are unreported, while 100 thousand tonnes, 34% of the total, are exported. In 2001, some of this 'unreported' waste appears to have been showing up – in the form of hospital and other hazardous waste – in illegal dumps in Wicklow, Dublin and elsewhere.

## Maintaining Environmental Standards and Competitiveness[5]

While the environmental demands on business have been steadily growing, there is no evidence that these are impairing competitiveness. In 1998 industry spent €150 million on environmental compliance measures associated with Integrated Pollution Control Licensing, comprising 19% of the total expenditure in that year.

**Table 7**
**Environmental Expenditure in Ireland, 1998 (€m)**

| Sector | Capital | Current | Total |
|---|---|---|---|
| Public | 141 | 270 | 411 |
| Industry | 93 | 58 | 151 |
| Agriculture | 43 | 172 | 216 |
| Energy | 11 | 4 | 15 |
| Total | 288 | 504 | 793 |

In chemicals and food processing, such outlays comprise on average 0.27% of total turnover, and, in general, this seems to be such a small percentage of turnover that it does not reduce competitiveness. But there may well be firms within these sectors who must spend more than the average, and who are marginal operators. The percentage of turnover (at 0.69%) is much higher for textiles, leather, pulp, paper and publishing. Unfortunately, the data available do not allow a finer breakdown of these sectors. Again, for sectors growing rapidly, as pulp and paper have been, compliance with the regulations is unlikely to pose a problem. The relatively high percentage may, however, pose a problem for the leather sector, which is already struggling and in decline.

## Lessons for the Future

The Irish have shown that, when we put our minds to it, we can achieve dramatic environmental improvement quickly. The clean-up of Dublin's air was helped very much by the natural shift from coal to natural gas as people's incomes rose, but it was also aided by an aggressive and successful policy – the ban on the marketing, sale and distribution of bituminous coal. Likewise, where a well-staffed organisation with a suitable legislative mandate and budget has been established with a clear brief, which is the situation as regards the Environmental Protection Agency and its integrated pollution control licensing, then even where industrial output doubles, it is possible to achieve absolute reductions in most emissions. But there is also evidence of 'environmental gombeenism' where the interests of tomorrow are compromised to facilitate today's fecklessness and self-indulgence.

There is an emerging problem with Ireland's environmental image at European level. There are several instances pending at various stages from complaint to court case, where the European Commission is challenging this country's compliance with EU Directives, either in terms of the timing of effort, its reach or its quality. The Irish strategy seems to be to stretch out the process for as long as possible, reaching compliance only at the point where court action is likely to result in decisions against the Irish position. There is considerable danger with this approach. If the perception takes hold among EU officials and EU-level non-governmental organisations that Ireland is being deliberately obstructive, this could eventually translate into a media image of Ireland as environmentally feckless, and this in turn could do great damage to those sectors of the economy, notably tourism and food, that depend on an image of environmental pristineness to give comparative advantage. As these sectors experience the cold winds of recession, it becomes imperative not to lose our high-quality environment image.

The main policy instrument being used to achieve environmental

## IS THE IRISH ECONOMY SUSTAINABLE?

Achieving sustainability, however defined, involves creating and maintaining wealth. There have been continuing efforts amongst economists to expand the concept of net savings and consequent changes in wealth by adjusting conventional measures to include changes in natural resource stocks, changes in health and education, and changes in wellbeing as a result of environmental degradation. A key underlying assumption of what is known as the 'weak sustainability' rule is that forms of capital are substitutes. This implies that a country could run down its natural capital but, if it were investing it in education and health, it could be considered sustainable. Genuine savings (GS) may be used as a measure of 'weak' sustainability and may be defined as: Gross Domestic Product (GDP) less consumption (C), depreciation (Dp), and depletion of natural assets (DI), plus investment in education (Ed) primary health (H) and research and development (RD) or:

$$GS = GDP - C - Dp - DI + Ed + H + RD$$

The World Bank has published estimates for 100 countries, which indicate that many developing countries fail the weak sustainability test, i.e. their net capital stock is in decline. Expressing these changes in per-capita terms for 1997, we find that Ireland's rapid growth gives it a high positive net savings rate, amounting to US$5,027. This leaves it ranked third in the world, behind Japan and Singapore! Because it has a relatively low natural resource endowment to draw down, and high rates of GDP growth and net private and public investment (including in the latter investment in education and health), Ireland shows a very positive balance in 'genuine saving'. However, the estimates of natural resource damage used do not include many of the significant environmental problems in Ireland. There is no real evidence of 'decoupling' economic growth from growth in emissions, although the rate of growth of the latter was much lower than the rate of growth of the economy. In addition, two key indicators of quality of urban life, traffic congestion and cost of accommodation, have deteriorated substantially and emissions of particulate matter and the increased incidence of noise complaints in cities are also of concern.

performance is direct investment. Tax incentives, either in the form of tax benefits, e.g. exemption from stamp duty on new houses that meet exceptional standards of energy efficiency, or charges, e.g. taxes on sulphur, carbon dioxide, are not used, nor is emissions trading. The absence of any positive or negative signals in the market place to encourage 'natural' environmental compliance is a significant weakness.[6] Emissions trading, in particular, has great potential to address a range of issues, including waste, as people are given permits to pollute, are allowed to trade them, and a 'price for using the environment' emerges.[7]

The economic slow-down will provide an opportunity to develop effective policies in those areas of environmental policy, notably waste and greenhouse gas emissions, where performance is poor and is being driven in the 'wrong' direction by economic growth.

# CHAPTER 11

# Climate Change and Energy

In an earlier chapter, we discussed the globalisation of economies. But globalisation of environmental concerns is also taking place, and this is linked to economic development. Specifically, as we have industrialised, we have increased our emissions of greenhouse gases, and this is thought to result in global warming. There is a rising concern about this phenomenon. Such concerns are difficult to understand viewed from a country where there is a lemming-like stampede south to the sun by as many as can afford it, and where an hour's sunshine sees pubs and restaurants trying to create an instant street-café society as tables and chairs are moved outside to take advantage of the 'solar gain'. And, in truth, such warming might not cause us many problems, and could indeed improve our situation as regards length of growing season and variety of crops produced.

Greenhouse gases keep the planet habitable. The main such gas is water vapour and clouds. It is noticeable in winter that a cloudless sky at night is colder than a cloudy one. The clouds reflect heat back to earth and keep us warmer. There are other greenhouse gases that we cannot see, and some of these are emitted mainly as a result of human effort. Notable among these latter greenhouse gases is carbon dioxide ($CO_2$) which is emitted as a by-product of fossil fuel energy consumption[1] and cement production. Since the industrial revolution, the amount of greenhouse gases emitted as a result of human activity

## CLIMATE CHANGE

The greenhouse effect is only one of several forces determining climatic development on earth, and it is directly related to the gas composition of the atmosphere, which has been an important climatic force throughout the planet's history. Certain gases, the greenhouse gases, allow short-wave sunlight to pass through the atmosphere but block the outgoing long-wave heat radiation from the earth. The most important greenhouse gas is water vapour ($H_2O$), followed by carbon dioxide ($CO_2$) and methane ($CH_4$). It is these gases that have made the earth habitable; the natural greenhouse effect increases the average temperature by 34°C. Without such gases, the earth would be a large uninhabitable snowball. Although water vapour is the most important greenhouse gas, it is usually disregarded when we talk about the total greenhouse effect because the content of water in the atmosphere is largely determined by climatic conditions, and is not governed by the release of water to the atmosphere from human activities. The enhanced or man-made greenhouse effect is caused mainly by human-induced emissions of $CO_2$ and other gases, that partially block a radiation window to the atmosphere that normally allows the earth to get rid of excessive heat. The greenhouse effect is particularly relevant in that it operates on a time-scale relevant to humans. Several of the other forces are noticeable only on much longer geological time scales.

It is important to note that the location of the emission of greenhouse gases is not significant in terms of environmental impact. For example, the emission of one tonne of gas in Australia does the same damage to Australians as does one tonne emitted in the USA. This is because the warming effect happens in the upper atmosphere. However, the results of the warming will vary depending on location, for example the Pacific islands are in danger of being submerged by rising sea levels.

Adapted from Knut H. Alfsen, 'Climate Change and Sustainability in Europe', *Achievement and Challenge – Ireland's Environmental Performance Assessed*, Edited by Frank J. Convery and John Feehan (forthcoming 2002) has risen, to the extent that the concentrations of such gases in the atmosphere has risen. Other greenhouse gases include: methane and nitrous oxide ($N_2O$), associated mainly with animal and crop production; chlorofluorocarbons (CFCs), formerly produced as a refrigerant and propellant, and implicated also in the depletion of the ozone layer; and two industrial gases – perfluorocarbons (PFCs) and sulphur hexafluoride ($SF_6$).

The rising concentrations of greenhouse gases in the atmosphere coincide with a rise in global temperatures, and this has led to the conclusion that there is likely to be a causal link between the two. Specifically, the jump since 1976 cannot be explained without taking man-made emissions into account.

## The Effects

So what if the planet gets warmer? The main problem is that playing God with the processes of nature seems a rash and risky thing to do. Hundreds of scientists have attempted to replicate nature using high-speed computers, and these simulations give us some idea as to what could lie ahead. In the northern hemisphere, winters are expected to get warmer, and rainfall generally will get more intense and droughts more enduring. One fairly predictable effect will be a sea-level rise, due to heating water and melting ice caps. If this happens, several island nations in the Pacific could disappear, and property along Sandymount strand in Dublin and other low-lying coastal areas could become less desirable than before, except for those with a preference for house-boats. Storm and flood damage will increase – this has already happened in some regions (Caribbean and Pacific); the malaria-prone zone will expand as warmer weather allows mosquitoes to invade more territory; there could be some expansion in agriculture and forestry as warmer weather expands the growing season and increased carbon in the atmosphere increases yields.[2] In Europe, it is expected that the south will experience the most dramatic effects, with more intense droughts (precipitation decreasing by up to 5% per decade) while northern Europe is expected to become warmer and wetter (precipitation increase of up to 2% per decade). Gale frequencies will possibly increase.[3]

While Europe and the developed world generally are likely to experience some negative effects as noted above, the developed world also has the resources, the technology and capacity to innovate as regards engineering, biology, insurance products etc. to adapt to such changes, even where, as they might, the changes occur very suddenly. In the developing world, where most of the planet's population resides, things are different. One 'weather event' can undo decades of economic development, and the overall effect of climate change is likely to increase the already widening gap between rich and poor.

## The Policy Response to Global Warming

The reality and prospect of rising temperatures has resulted in efforts at international level to stabilise and then reduce human-induced emissions of greenhouse gases. The problem was first recognised at the level of international policy at the UN conference on environment and development that took place in Stockholm in 1972. This led to the establishment in 1988 of the Intergovernmental Panel on Climate Change (IPCC) to assess current scientific knowledge and suggest remedies. The UN Conference on Environment and Development – the Rio Earth Summit – produced the UN Framework Convention on Climate Change (UNFCCC), which was signed by the participants, and recognised, in a non-binding fashion, the need for industrialised countries to control their emissions of greenhouse gases. This, in turn, was followed by the Kyoto Protocol in 1997, where binding greenhouse-gas emission targets were set for industrialised countries. These international efforts have translated into specific concrete commitments in the Kyoto Protocol, which have been agreed by the EU, Japan, Canada and Australia, but not the US. Under a burden-sharing agreement, as a

**THE DIFFERENCE BETWEEN GLOBAL WARMING
AND THE HOLE IN THE OZONE LAYER**

The ozone layer in the stratosphere absorbs ultraviolet light. Ozone depletion is a process whereby CFCs (which are artificial products manufactured to provide refrigeration and aerosol propellants) are released into the atmosphere, and there they break down the ozone layer. If we receive too much ultraviolet light, it increases the incidence of skin cancer, and could damage the productivity of our oceans. An 'ozone hole' was discovered in 1985 by the British Antarctic Survey, and this accelerated progress towards phasing out the production and use of CFCs.

Global warming is the process whereby human-induced emissions of greenhouse gases to the atmosphere are intensifying 'natural' global warming. The only relationship between these is that CFCs, in addition to their role in depleting the ozone layer, are also themselves greenhouse gases.

member of the European Union, Ireland has accepted an annual quota (expressed in tonnes of carbon dioxide equivalent) to be achieved by 2008–2012.

**Making money while reducing global warming**: The Kyoto Protocol has a number of very innovative ways, called 'flexible mechanisms', for making the reduction of emissions of greenhouse gases profitable. Three such mechanisms are recognised as valid means towards meeting targets: emissions trading, Joint Implementation (JI), and the Clean Development Mechanism (CDM).

In the case of emissions trading, quotas of greenhouse gases are allocated to emitters, and their emissions must not exceed the amount of the quota they hold. But if they find it very expensive to stay within their quota, they can buy additional quota from others who can reduce emissions below their quota at low cost, hence the term 'flexible mechanism'. Milk quotas work exactly the same way in Ireland. Farmers who want to produce more milk for sale than they have quota for have to buy quota from other farmers who are reducing their production for sale. The total volume of milk sold does not change. Similarly, the total 'envelope' of emissions remains the same, but, by allowing emissions to be traded, those who can reduce their emissions at least cost do so, and sell on their unused quota to those for whom reduction is more expensive. The costs on the economy of meeting the target are thereby minimised. The local impact from climate change does not depend on the geographical source of emissions, hence if Ireland were to buy emissions quota from another country this would not worsen the Irish environment. The European Commission has proposed that an EU-wide trading scheme be in place by 2005, and countries outside the EU have agreed that a global trading scheme will be in place by 2008.

With joint implementation, industrialised countries can undertake projects in other industrialised countries (it is expected that such investment will flow mainly from the richer OECD group to poorer industrialised countries such as Russia and the countries of the former Soviet bloc) and the reductions in appropriately accredited projects can be claimed by the investor in the project.

The Clean Development Mechanism (CDM) operates in a manner similar to joint implementation, except that it applies in developing countries. There is provision for the use of carbon sinks, mainly forests (trees absorb and store carbon for a long period) established since 1990, as a contribution to meeting the emissions target or quota.

Negotiations on how to apply the regulatory frameworks for these mechanisms and carbon sinks broke down in The Hague in late 2000, and the US announced that it was withdrawing from the Kyoto process entirely. But further negotiation in Bonn in the summer of 2001 resulted in political agreement to proceed without the US. Restrictions on emissions trading proposed at The Hague by the EU were eliminated, and the absorption of emissions by forests was given greater weight. This facilitated agreement on how to implement the Kyoto Protocol at Marrakech in November 2001.

**AGREEMENT AT MARRAKECH, NOVEMBER 2001 –
THE GLOBAL WARMING PLAN OF ACTION**

Despite the withdrawal of the US from the process, the other parties to the Kyoto Protocol agreed on the implementation of the process. The agreement covered:

➤ International emissions trading to start in 2008.

➤ Mechanisms for ensuring compliance across countries.

➤ Monitoring and reporting mechanisms established to provide transparency and certainty for the operation of the Kyoto mechanisms.

➤ Provision for immediate start of the Clean Development Mechanism (CDM).

➤ From 2008 on, implementation of Joint Implementation projects.

➤ Provision for linkage between assigned amount units (the initial national allocations), the removal units earned from sequestration, the units earned from CDM and Joint Implementation projects, which can be transferred between the parties without restriction.

➤ Rules for the use of credits from sink activities in forestry and agriculture. Russia secured a special allocation of 33 million tonnes of $CO_2$-equivalent.

The EU and Japan played key roles with 'the excellent relationship' between Commissioner Wallström and Japanese Minister Kawaguchi being a major asset.

## The Impacts of Implementing the Kyoto Protocol

Our projections here indicate that even if the Kyoto Protocol is fully implemented, it will have a very trivial effect on global warming. This is because the US has 'dropped out', developing countries are not included (rapidly growing coal-based economies in India and China are increasing emissions), the targets agreed are modest relative to the challenge, and there is great inertia in the system in that $CO_2$ has a residence time of well over fifty years, so that action taken today changes outcomes only in the next generation. Why bother? The rationale is simple: we need to start somewhere and Kyoto is at present the only game in town.

## The Irish Response

Under the provisions of the Kyoto Protocol, the EU agreed to a quota (3922 million tonnes of $CO_2$-equivalent for the Union) comprising a reduction of 8% below 1990 levels for the six greenhouse gases. In June 1998 a system of burden-sharing or target-sharing was agreed for the EU member states, and to meet this aggregate target each member state was allocated its own quota. Ireland's target or quota is about 61 million tonnes of $CO_2$-equivalent – 13% above the 1990 level.

The problem for Ireland in general, and industry in particular, is that under 'business as usual' we will not meet this target. If we experience a sustained recession – lasting for over two years – this is likely to 'solve' some of our problem, as fossil fuel use is so closely related to economic growth. But if recovery takes place within eighteen months or less, then we have a substantial 'overshoot' to deal with.[4]

## The Energy Issue

Energy is intimately linked to climate change because when you burn coal, oil, gas, peat – any fuel that contains carbon – the carbon is released and combines with oxygen in the atmosphere to produce carbon dioxide ($CO_2$), the main greenhouse gas. Growth in the economy and in energy consumption has resulted in a rapid increase in greenhouse gas emissions, to the extent that the 13% increase above the 1990 baseline has already been exceeded in 2000. Under 'business as usual' the overshoot is expected to amount to at least 5 million tonnes by 2010,[5] even allowing for the contribution of over 3 million tonnes of $CO_2$-equivalent contributed by 'carbon sinks', attributable to afforestation.

**Table 8**

**Greenhouse Gas Emissions (thousand tonnes of $CO_2$-equivalent)**

| Gas | 1990 | 2000 | 2005 | 2010 |
|---|---|---|---|---|
| $CO_2$ | 32,159 | 43,359 | 47,130 | 48,914 |
| Methane | 12,836 | 11,666 | 11,590 | 11,081 |
| Nitrous Oxide | 9086 | 9629 | 9673 | 9719 |
| Sinks | 0 | -893 | -2013 | -3008 |
| Total | 54,081 | 63,642 | 65,387 | 65,571 |
| Change on 1990 (%) | 0.0 | 17.7 | 20.9 | 21.2 |

Nearly all the growth is attributable to increases in carbon-dioxide emissions, associated mainly with rising fossil-fuel consumption, and to a lesser extent cement production. Methane and nitrous oxide are produced mainly by agriculture, and little growth is envisaged from this source.

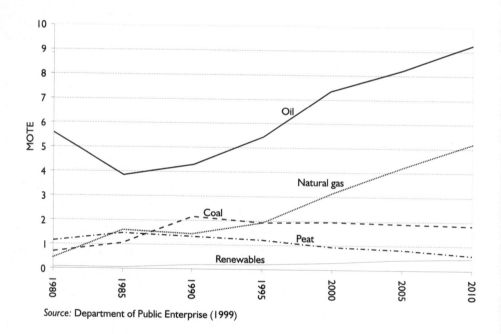

*Source:* Department of Public Enterprise (1999)

Figure 19: TOTAL PRIMARY ENERGY REQUIREMENTS BY FUEL TYPE
(MILLION TONNES OF OIL-EQUIVALENT, 1980–2010)

But there are other reasons besides climate change to reduce our dependence on fossil fuels. Serious money is spent on energy in Ireland. According to the Irish Energy Centre, this amounted in 2000 to €6336 million, comprising expenditure on energy for transport (€3682 million), agriculture (€114 million), housing (€1140 million), tertiary (€762 million), industry (€635 million).[5] Ireland and its territorial waters have so far proved relatively barren as regards commercial deposits of oil, gas and coal, with only small commercial gas fields at Kinsale Head – the original, and a new one likely to come on stream – and the Corrib field in the Atlantic off the coast of Mayo. There are small commercial deposits of peat, and larger non-commercial deposits[6] being exploited for electricity production. Figure 19 summarises the situation as regards the balance of Irish energy supply. Dominated by oil and natural gas, followed by coal – explained mainly by coal use in the Electricity Supply Board's (ESB's) coal-fired plant at Moneypoint, County Clare – then peat, with renewables taking up a very minor share. Figure 19 also shows how energy consumption is influenced by the level of economic activity: there was a fall in total primary energy requirements in the mid-1980s when the economy was in deep recession, manufacturing plants were closing, and people were selling their cars and turning off the central heating.

The recovery in the 1990s is reflected in rapidly growing energy consumption, dominated by oil and natural gas, with a sharp step-wise growth over the 1995–2000 period coincident with the most rapid growth the Irish economy has ever experienced.

It makes sense to reduce our energy bill where the value of the savings made is greater than the costs incurred, for example, the extra cost of buying a more efficient machine. Many of our leading companies have recognised the merits of this logic, and achieved dramatic energy savings over the past five years.

We could all achieve big reductions in energy consumption in our houses, workplaces and cars if we took the time and effort to do so. Why don't we? There are two explanations. The first is that we are ignorant about the opportunities we have; the second is that it is not

155

## SELF AUDITING IN IRELAND

The Irish Energy Centre operates a self-audit scheme for the top energy consumers (spending not less than €1.27 million per annum on energy). The companies that chose to participate account for 35% of all energy consumed by the industrial sector. The scheme provides assistance on monitoring use of energy and setting reduction targets; companies commit publicly to a reduction target and report their experiences regularly, and help one another through various networking, workshop and related mechanisms. The top ten performers – out of the total number of companies (76) participating – are listed below in the Energy Performance Index, to a base of 100 in 1995 or 1996.

| Company | 1995/96 | Actual in 2000 | Target 2001 |
|---|---|---|---|
| 1. Waterford Crystal | 100 | 37 | 37 |
| 2. Norvatis Ringaskiddy | 100 | 43 | 40 |
| 3. Glaxo Smithkline Cork | 100 | 51 | 49 |
| 4. Janssen Pharmaceuticals | 100 | 51 | 51 |
| 5. Garrett Engineering | 100 | 52 | 49 |
| 6. Intel Ireland | 100 | 59 | 57 |
| 7. Buckeye Technologies | 100 | 60 | 60 |
| 8. Klinge Pharma | 100 | 61 | 56 |
| 9. Schering Plough | 100 | 62 | 59 |
| 10. De Beers Industrial Diamonds | 100 | 64 | 58 |

Irish Energy Centre, *Annual Self-Audit and Statement of Energy Accounts Scheme, 2000–2001*, Dublin, pp. 15–17

worth the money and hassle involved to us. As regards the latter, there is nothing like financial pressure and a crisis to trigger action. It was the energy crises of 1973 to 1974 and 1978 to 1979 that drove the development of the very efficient combined-cycle gas turbines (CCGT) for electricity generators, the development to near commerciality of wind power, advances in combined heat and power technologies, and intensified integration of energy supply systems, mainly via gas pipelines and electricity interconnectors. Such developments reduce energy intensity – the amount of energy used per unit of GDP.

In addition to spending a lot of money on energy, we are very dependent on oil imports – they comprise about two-thirds of our energy imports. And the problem for us all is that the cheapest and most plentiful oil is located in very volatile regions of the world. Specifically, there are vast deposits (comprising over 70% of proven reserves) of oil in the Middle East where costs of extraction are the lowest in the world (about $1 or less per barrel) and it is by exploiting this storehouse that we are guaranteed the low-cost energy that we enjoy today. Venezuela and Russia are next in size. The share of the total held by Western Europe is less than 2%. There are considerable stores remaining in other parts of the world and other reserves yet to be discovered, but they will involve relatively high-cost extraction. Stores of natural gas are likewise geographically concentrated, with North Africa (Algeria), Russia and the North Sea being prominent in this regard. Reserves of coal are more ubiquitous, with Australia, South America, the US, China and parts of Europe all well endowed.

The 'oil age' will not run out of oil, any more than the Stone Age ran out of stone. But because of the geography of the location of oil there are likely to be supply interruptions, and these in turn are likely to lead to extreme price volatility from time to time. And Ireland is uniquely vulnerable to such perturbations.

Fortunately, we have some strong cards to play as regards improving our energy performance. Notably, we have what many regard as the best wind regime in Europe, and we have barely tapped into this resource. Our relative inaction as regards energy conservation, notably as regards households, commercial and transport, means that there is much we can achieve at relatively low cost, and the Irish Energy Centre is now geared up to move this agenda forward.

## TAKING ADVANTAGE OF THE WIND IN THE IRISH SEA

'A foreshore lease has been signed permitting the development of what is expected to be the world's largest wind farm, off the East Coast of Ireland, on the Arklow Bank, which is seven to ten km off shore. The bank is 24km long, 2.5km wide, with water depth ranging from 5 to 25 metres along its length. The farm will cover 24 hectares, and will comprise 200 turbines, each 110 metres high. The cost will exceed €630 million, and it is hoped that 60 megawatts (MW) will be installed by the third quarter of 2002. The total capacity to be installed will amount to 520 MW, which compares with 1200 MW at the coal fired plant at Moneypoint, County Clare, the largest generating station in Ireland. Eddie O'Connor, Managing Director of Eirtricity, the company developing the farm, is quoted as saying: "The resource is there, the technology is proven, the costs continue to drop – all that is needed is the political will to see it happen." Potential impacts on bird life and fisheries are said by Birdwatch Ireland and fisheries organisations to be unknown.'

'Government signs deal for world's largest wind farm off Irish coast', by Lorna Siggins, *The Irish Times*, 12 January 2002, p.19.

## Lessons for the Future

The climate-change problem is not going to go away. It is likely that increasingly aberrant storms, flooding, droughts and other catastrophes will keep the issue on the agenda, even if the Kyoto process fails. The effects in proportionate terms will be felt mainly in the developing world. The rich North will be able to make the investments and innovations needed to provide adaptation and protection. Thus the issue is a parable for the North–South divide, and may prove one more resentment to add to the list of triggers that fuel discontentment in developing countries.

There is no 'silver bullet' at present available that would allow a large low-cost reduction in greenhouse gas emissions. The only currently available options are energy conservation and fuel switching from more carbon intensive (coal and oil) to less carbon intensive (natural gas) or zero carbon (wind) energy sources.

**MORE PRICE TURBULENCE IN THE FUTURE**

'Fifteen of the nineteen men who hijacked four planes on 11 September were Saudis, as is Osama bin Laden. According to Larry Goldstein, President of the Petroleum Industry Research Association, "The political situation is coming to a head and not just in the Middle East. The next ten years will be more volatile in terms of price than the last ten."'

Nelson D. Schwartz, 'Breaking OPEC's Grip', *Fortune,* Europe Edition, No. 23, November 19 2001, p.53

The 2001–2002 recession will reduce the growth in energy consumption. If the recession is sustained and severe, it will result in absolute reductions in energy consumption. This, in turn, will provide a 'breathing space' to bring Irish emissions into compliance with our Kyoto quota (not that we feel supressing economic growth is the appropriate way to resolve our 'overshoot' problem). The 'overshoot' is now estimated at only about 5 million tonnes of $CO_2$-equivalent.

With oil comprising close on two-thirds of our final energy consumption, Ireland has extreme and growing vulnerability to interruptions in oil supply, and/or escalations in its price. Events in the US at the end of 2001 prove the truism that 'history is always a surprise'. From an energy and economy point of view, one of the most unpleasant surprises would be some combination of military and political upheaval in the Middle East, notably Saudi Arabia, that reduced oil supplies to world markets to the point at which prices escalated. Such escalation would be self-correcting in the medium term, as sharp price rises are likely to intensify global recessionary forces, and these will reduce consumption, which, in turn, will reduce pressure on prices. But in the meantime, everyone will suffer, and Ireland will suffer in particular as a consequence of our unusually high oil dependence.

What we must *not* do is introduce price controls. This is tempting because an oil company that has loaded a tanker at $20 a barrel, and finds that after it has left harbour prices have jumped to $60 a barrel will achieve an enormous capital gain. But such shipments will flow to wherever is paying the top price; price control below world prices will guarantee scarcity and queues.

We need to have hedging arrangements in place, so that rapid upward price movements are mitigated for companies by having bought forward. We need to have a 'rapid reaction' energy conservation programme, such that there is both an immediate and a medium-term slow-down of consumption. The Irish Energy Centre website (www.irish-energy.ie) lists a variety of such interventions. For example, for Home Energy Management interventions that are costless, the menu includes: turning down thermostats, using timers, switching off lights when not needed, switching from the use of open fires, taking showers rather than baths, only leaving windows open and extractor fans on in winter when necessary to provide sufficient fresh air and avoid build up of moisture, closing curtains at night and, when rooms are heated by sun, opening internal doors to distribute heat, leaving space behind fridges so that coils will not overheat, defrosting freezer regularly, using lowest water temperature required for dishwasher and using with full loads, when washing in sink using stopper rather than leaving hot water running. Further menus are provided for interventions that cost around €100 (insulating hot-water heater, draught-sealing doors and windows, improving heating and hot-water controls, using energy efficient lamps [compact fluorescent lamps], insulating curtains and window boards, fitting reflective foils on back of radiators on wall side).

Finally, we need a 'fast track' implementation of the renewables programme. We have benefited by delaying, because the costs, especially of wind power, have fallen so sharply over the past two decades. But we can now move, with very low costs in terms of competitiveness loss, as the gap has narrowed dramatically.

Emissions trading is likely to be the most effective and promising short-term solution to the Irish 'overshoot' of the Kyoto greenhouse gas quota. The US had been expected to be a substantial buyer of

## WINDS OF CHANGE

'DaimlerChrysler's New Electric Car Version 5 (Necar 5) represents the company's $1 billion bet on the car of the future. It produces one-third less carbon dioxide than a conventional car, and its performance is that of a gasoline powered Mercedes A Class. It uses methanol, which is liquid at normal temperatures, and can be produced from gas or wood, and can be transported, stored and pumped like gasoline. The methanol goes into a reformer, which extracts hydrogen, which in turn powers a fuel cell, which runs the electric motor. Fuel cells are essentially batteries whose power is derived from the constant inflow of some form of fuel. The first fuel cell cars are scheduled to go on sale in 2004, and will probably cost 10% more than their conventional counterparts.'

\* \* \*

'Two hundred BP filling stations in ten countries are fitted with see-through canopies above the pumps called 'thin film' that absorbs sunlight and turns it into sufficient electricity – even on a dull English day – to run the pumps and keep the lights on. Thin film consists of semiconductor circuits no thicker than a hair that are deposited directly on glass. The global solar industry is growing at 20% per year, with revenues in 2000 of $1.5 billion. It will be at least a decade before it becomes economically competitive with conventional sources. The cost of solar energy in Europe is about 20 cent to 25 cent per kilowatt hour, much more than conventional energy. But costs have fallen by 50% in the past decade, and the learning curve is expected to continue to drive prices down. "Solar's great strength," says BP group vice president, Andrew Mackenzie, "is its acceptability."'

\* \* \*

'In the 1990s, Denmark made the breakthroughs that have dramatically changed the economics of wind energy. The best wind turbines can now produce a kilo-watt hour of electricity (enough to light ten 100 watt bulbs for an hour) for as little as 5 cent – half the cost five years ago, and one fifth the cost in 1980. That could fall to 4 cent in 2004, making wind power almost as cheap as fossil fuels, which typically cost 3 cent to 4 cent per kilowatt hour. Fifteen percent of all electricity is generated from renewables, and this is projected to rise to 20% by 2003. The new wind frontier is the shallow seas off the

161

coast of Denmark, where winds are steadier and stronger, adding 50% to their energy content. The newest off-shore turbines have rotors with a diameter of up to 230 feet, longer than the wing span of a Boeing 747. Five nations – Denmark, Germany, US, Spain, India – account for 80% of the world's turbines. Revenues reached $4.5 billion in 2000. Danish companies have over 50% of the world market, but ABB of Sweden is planning a test of a turbine called Windformer that it says will revolutionise the industry because of its simpler components and the ability to transmit electricity over longer distances.'

Henry Muller, 'Winds of Change', *Fortune*, Europe Edition, No. 6, 26 March 2001, pp. 30–40

emissions quota. With this purchasing power out of the market, it is expected that the price of the quota will be very low, perhaps as low as four dollars a tonne of $CO_2$-equivalent. If the Irish overshoot is of the order of 5 million tonnes, this implies that the deficit could be purchased for as little as $20 million annually. This compares with a current annual outlay of €150 million ($168 million) on environmental protection by Irish industry at present.[7] Although this price signal will be low, relative to what would have prevailed with the US in, it will still send a message that there is money to be made if $CO_2$-emissions can be reduced at a cost of less than $4 per tonne. If the challenge to address the global warming issue is seriously tackled in the future, then quotas will be reduced and their value increased.

It will be a strategic challenge for industry to identify low-cost carbon reduction opportunities and act upon them as soon as the emerging price signal justifies such investment. It would be worthwhile identifying the opportunities associated with different $CO_2$ price scenarios, ranging from $4 to $30 per tonne. For example, if quota are priced nearer $30 it will become more cost-effective to invest in reducing emissions rather than buying the quota. It will also be more worthwhile to invest in innovation.

Europe seems to have a lead in a number of energy-efficient and alternative energy technologies. So far, as regards participating in the development of technology and its manufacture, Irish industry seems to have missed out completely. It is important that Irish enterprise be aware of latest developments, and of the potential to participate in new initiatives.

The measures involving greenhouse gases will reinforce the measures encouraging energy conservation noted above. These will include some combination of voluntary approaches, carbon taxes and emissions trading. Europe is leading the world in the development of alternative energy systems and technologies. It is important that Irish companies, which may have some comparative advantage in such areas, participate in R&D so that they can participate in these new growth areas. The Irish Energy Centre intends to manage an energy research programme that will help develop comparative advantage in such areas.

# CHAPTER 12

# Quality of Life

*'Nobody in Ireland will be happy until everybody is better off than everybody else.'*
*John B. Keane*

*'Those who say that money can't buy happiness don't know where to shop.' Anon* [1]

*'Happiness is nothing more than good health and a bad memory.' Albert Schweitzer*

Economists are often perceived by the general public as being interested only in money. This is not surprising, given the frequency with which city types pop up on television to predict the impact on the markets of the latest piece of economic data. This notion of where the interests of economists lie is also the view of many policy makers. Indeed, the economist Paul Krugman of Massachusetts Institute of Technology (MIT) states that members of his profession tend to be consulted on those things of which they know least (see box opposite). It will by now be apparent to our readers that economists concern themselves with much more than just macroeconomic variables such as GDP, inflation and interest rates. Economics is a social science and, at the end of the day, applied economics and policy analysis are all about trying to find ways to improve human well-being. Indeed, a common definition of economics is that it

**MURPHY'S LAW OF ECONOMIC POLICY**

Paul Krugman of MIT defines Murphy's Law of economic policy: 'Economists have the least influence on policy when they know the most and are most agreed [for example, on increasing the competitiveness of markets, such as the deregulation of the taxi market and the opening up of air access to competition]; they have the most influence when they know the least and disagree most vehemently [such as predicting future stock prices, interest rates and exchange rates]. So now you know why economists are useless: when they actually understand something, people don't want to hear about it.'

Paul Krugman, 'See Why Economists are Useless', *International Herald Tribune*, 8 June 2000

studies how to maximise human welfare in the presence of constraints – and the most important constraints are the ways humans respond to incentives.

However, while economics textbooks talk about 'utility' and 'welfare', we do not have handy ways of measuring them and so, in discussing economic progress, economists are usually seen in the media talking about growth rates in terms of GDP and GNP. Nevertheless, despite the perceptions, economists do realise that changes in such measures are not perfect reflections of changes in the welfare of society. These measures ignore, for the most part, many aspects of quality of life such as the natural environment within which people live, civil rights, and social cohesion and the fabric of society generally. Economists are also aware that there is, at best, a weak association between the growth of GDP and how 'happy' people feel. But given the choice, most people would prefer to be wealthier rather than poorer, and they do feel better off when their standard of living is rising rapidly. It is also true that unemployment is closely linked to unhappiness. While great strides have been made in the application of economics to environmental issues, economists have tended to shy away from exploring other variables that affect human well-being, mainly because of the difficulty of measuring them quantitatively. This chapter examines the determinants that Irish people perceive to

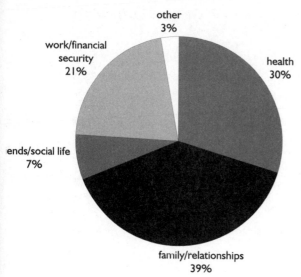

other
3%

work/financial
security
21%

health
30%

ends/social life
7%

family/relationships
39%

Figure 20: THE MOST IMPORTANT THING IN THE LIVES OF
IRISH PEOPLE, 2001

be of most importance with regard to the quality of their lives and examines the effect of economic growth on determinants of well-being.

## What are the most important considerations in Irish people's lives?

To answer this question, we rely on a survey of 1500 Irish adults carried out in spring 2001 for the Urban Institute in University College Dublin.[2] Respondents were asked to state what they considered to be 'the most important thing' in their lives. Family and relationships were most frequently cited (39%) followed by health (30%). Work and financial security were considered the most important by 2 out of 10 people (Figure 20).

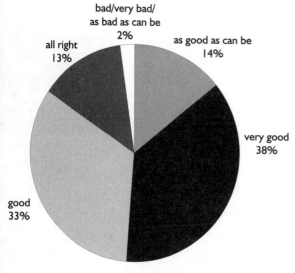

bad/very bad/
as bad as can be
2%

all right
13%

as good as can be
14%

very good
38%

good
33%

Figure 21: IRISH PEOPLE'S RATING OF THEIR LIFE AS A
WHOLE, 2001

## How do Irish people rate their lives as a whole?

Levels of satisfaction among the population regarding their lives as a whole are generally high. For example, well over two-thirds consider that their lives are either 'very good' or 'good', with a further 14% describing their lives as 'as good as can be'. (Figure 21).

## How do the Irish rate their lives in comparison to other Europeans?

The findings of the UCD survey are supported by the Eurobarometer data in Figure 22 which show 9 out of 10 Irish people 'very satisfied' or 'satisfied' with their lives. These levels of satisfaction are very similar to those reported in Sweden, the Netherlands and the UK. The Danes seem to be the most content nation in the EU, while the Greeks are the least content with only 6 out of every 10 people being satisfied. Overall, Ireland lies in the middle of the EU happiness league table, ranking joint seventh with Belgium out of the fifteen EU member states. It is interesting to compare the satisfaction rates of the Irish with the other Cohesion countries of the EU – Greece, Portugal and Spain (these countries plus Ireland were classified as Cohesion countries because their GDP *per capita* was significantly below the EU average). Four out of 10 Greeks are dissatisfied with their lives, as are a third of the Portuguese and 17% of the Spanish. Of the Cohesion countries, the Irish are the most content with life with just 12% rating their lives as unsatisfactory (a good climate does not seem

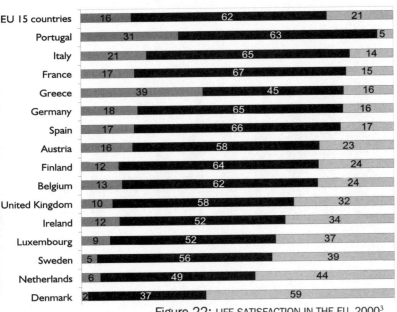

Figure 22: LIFE SATISFACTION IN THE EU, 2000[3]

to be all that important after all!). However, care must be taken when comparing countries, as we note later.

## Has economic progress improved life satisfaction?

Looking over time, it seems that the Irish became more satisfied with their lot as the economy boomed. Figure 23 suggests that more Irish people were dissatisfied with their lives during the 1980s than in the proceeding and preceding decades. This might be explained by the prolonged recession in the 1980s and the associated unemployment level. However, the data also show that the Irish were more happy in the 1970s when GDP *per capita* was considerably lower than today. Out of the nine countries, only in the Netherlands, France and Italy has life satisfaction increased in each decade. If the figures for 2000 reflect the 1990s, on average, there has been no change in life satisfaction in the nine European countries in three decades. This appears to be consistent with results from the US which show that happiness with life appears to be increasing, but the rise is so small that it seems

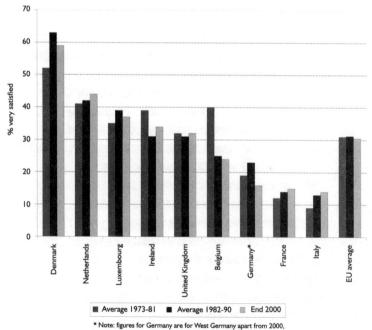

Figure 23: LIFE SATISFACTION IN SELECTED EU COUNTRIES 1973–81, 1982–90, 2000[4]

that extra income is not contributing dramatically to raising people's feeling of happiness.[5] There may be a closer correlation with the unemployment rate than with the level of GDP.

## What factors influence the happiness of Irish people?

We know the rich are different from us – they have more money – but are they happier? A simple analysis of the UCD Urban Institute survey shows that happiness does vary by social class, but the association with class is not very close. There is not much difference between the four 'higher' social classes from A to C2, but there is a sharp fall off in happiness in the 'lowest' classes. In categories D and E, just 7 out of 10 and 6 out of 10 respectively rate their lives as satisfactory compared to about 9 out of 10 in the other classes (Figure 24).

This may be because the risk of unemployment is so high lower down the social ordering and there is a strong relationship between employment status and happiness. Figure 25 shows that 95% of the self employed, 91% of the full-time employees, 86% of those who are

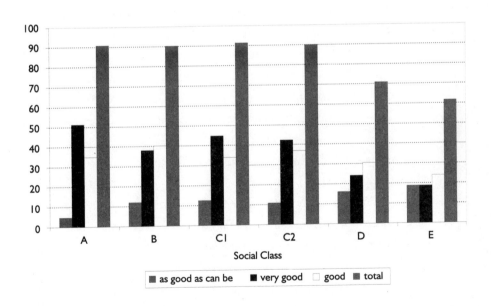

Social Class

as good as can be  ■ very good  good  ■ total

Figure 24: LIFE SATISFACTION BY SOCIAL CLASS, 2001

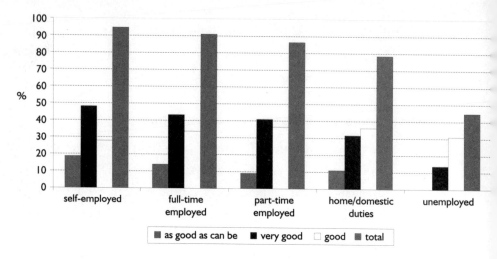

Figure 25: IRISH PEOPLE'S RATING OF THEIR LIVES BY EMPLOYMENT STATUS, 2001

employed part-time, and 79% of those who work in the home are satisfied with their lives. However, only 45% of those who are unemployed rate their lives as satisfactory. Such results have also been shown for other European countries. We might be justified in concluding that maintaining full employment rather than maximising incomes is what matters from a policy perspective.

However, care must be taken in comparing countries. Just because one country has a higher unemployment rate than another country does not *necessarily* mean that its population as a whole is less happy. This is because cultural and historical factors influence people's happiness. This shows the complexity of assessing those factors that influence life satisfaction and the difficulty of making inter-country comparisons.

There is barely any significant difference between Irish males and females in terms of life satisfaction. However, religious belief does seem to matter. Those who believe in God express a slightly higher satisfaction with life than non-believers (Figure 26) although only 7% of the population declare themselves to be non-believers.

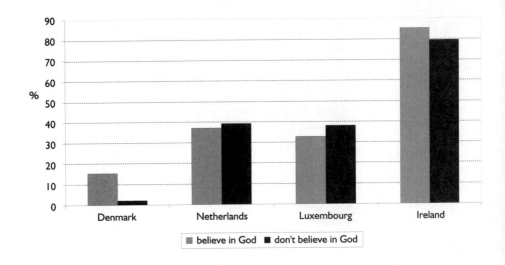

Figure 26: IRISH PEOPLE'S RATING OF THEIR LIVES BY BELIEF IN GOD, 2001

## Do Irish people feel better off than in the past?

'The past is another country; they do things differently there.' So said L. P. Hartley. Care has to be taken in the interpretation of answers to questions about how we felt in the past – maybe we see it through rose-tinted glasses? But the UCD Urban Institute survey shows that one in two Irish people considered themselves 'better off' in spring 2001 than they were two years before. Moreover, a slightly higher proportion considered themselves better off than five years previously (Figure 27). This is likely to be a reflection of the growth in the Irish economy and the fall in unemployment during the 1990s. Only one in ten people believed they were worse off in summer 2001 than two or five years ago. But, as we have seen, while feeling 'better off' people do not seem to feel 'more satisfied with life'.

## How has the Celtic Tiger affected the most important issues in people's lives?

Those taking part in the UCD survey were asked how the record growth of the Irish economy in the past ten years affected things most

171

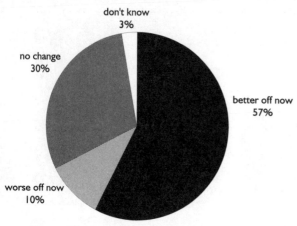

Figure 27: OPINION OF IRISH PUBLIC AS TO WHETHER THEY ARE BETTER OR WORSE OFF THAN 5 YEARS AGO, 2001

important to them. Similar proportions stated that it had either 'improved' (47%) or 'made no difference to' (44%) the most important things in their lives. Only a small number of people felt that the rapid growth in the Irish economy had either 'greatly improved' or 'greatly deteriorated' the most important things in their lives (Figure 28).

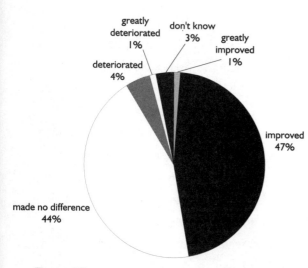

Figure 28: OPINION OF IRISH PUBLIC OF CELTIC TIGER'S EFFECT ON THE IMPORTANT THINGS IN THEIR LIVES, 2001

## What has been the impact of the Celtic Tiger on the factors that influence quality of life?

As expected, the vast majority of respondents to the survey believed that the Celtic Tiger had either 'improved' or 'greatly improved' the economy. Over half felt that the tax system had improved. However, respondents felt that a number of issues had also deteriorated in Ireland. Predictably, traffic congestion was considered to have 'deteriorated' or 'greatly deteriorated' by 6 out of 10 people. A third felt the Irish had become less friendly. Almost three-quarters considered that the drugs situation had deteriorated (Table 9).

**Table 9**

**Opinion of the Irish Public Concerning the Impact of the 'Celtic Tiger' Economy on Various Issues, 2001**

| | Greatly Improved | Improved | Made No Difference | Deteriorated | Greatly Deteriorated | Don't Know |
|---|---|---|---|---|---|---|
| | % | % | % | % | % | % |
| Public Transport | 6 | 32 | 50 | 4 | 4 | 4 |
| Safety | 2 | 12 | 38 | 38 | 8 | 2 |
| Personal Safety | 1 | 10 | 54 | 30 | 4 | 1 |
| Crime | 1 | 10 | 54 | 30 | 4 | 1 |
| Friendliness of People | 2 | 12 | 53 | 27 | 5 | 1 |
| Drugs | 1 | 5 | 20 | 43 | 28 | 3 |
| Traffic Congestion | 1 | 5 | 12 | 33 | 47 | 2 |
| Economy | 24 | 51 | 17 | 3 | 2 | 3 |
| Health | 4 | 27 | 54 | 9 | 3 | 3 |
| Environment | 4 | 28 | 39 | 19 | 5 | 5 |
| Technology | 35 | 41 | 15 | 2 | 1 | 6 |
| Immigration | 8 | 38 | 31 | 9 | 4 | 10 |
| People with Disabilities | 3 | 28 | 41 | 7 | 5 | 16 |
| Taxes | 7 | 50 | 27 | 6 | 2 | 8 |
| Politics | 2 | 12 | 39 | 19 | 15 | 13 |
| Irish Travellers | 3 | 17 | 54 | 8 | 4 | 14 |

## Health status of the Irish population

Given that health was most frequently cited as the most important thing in the lives of the Irish, perception of health status is of great relevance to quality of life. Some 1 in 5 considered that their health was 'excellent' and a further 4 out of 10 that it was 'very good'. Only 2% felt that their health was 'poor' (Figure 29). (Of course, those in hospitals and nursing homes were not included in our sample!)

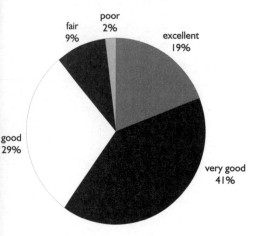

Although 8 out of 10 people in the Social Class A ('highest') category describe their health as either excellent or very good, the equivalent figure for those in Social Class D is only 4 out of 10 (Figure 30).

## Anxiety, Worry and Suicide

It is often suggested that economic growth can lead to a faster pace of life which, allied to increased stress caused by such things as over-work and traffic congestion, can lead to anxiety and depression. The UCD survey shows that, in spite of higher incomes and lower unemployment, people are still likely to feel continual anxiety regarding money issues, work and job security. People are

Figure 29: SELF-REPORTED HEALTH STATUS OF THE IRISH POPULATION, 2001

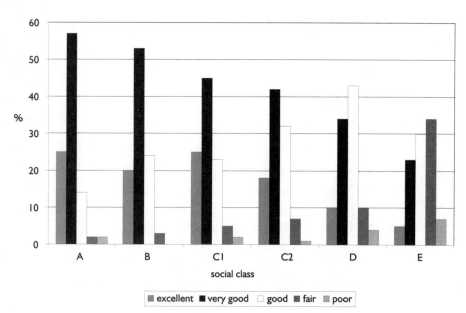

Figure 30: SELF-REPORTED HEALTH STATUS BY SOCIAL CLASS, 2001

174

more than twice as likely to worry about housing than they are about the global environment (Table 10).

**Table 10**
**Issues Which Cause Degrees of Anxiety to the Irish Public, 2001**

|  | Never | A Little | Some-times | All the Time |
|---|---|---|---|---|
|  | % | % | % | % |
| Your Physical Health | 45 | 30 | 20 | 5 |
| Your Mental/Emotional Health | 70 | 16 | 11 | 3 |
| Your Children's Health | 23 | 35 | 34 | 8 |
| Your Personal Safety | 32 | 38 | 25 | 5 |
| Money | 21 | 37 | 25 | 17 |
| Work/Job Security | 39 | 27 | 23 | 11 |
| Housing | 58 | 18 | 18 | 6 |
| Global Environment | 45 | 33 | 19 | 3 |

There is considerable concern in Ireland regarding the rising suicide rate amongst young males. Figure 31 shows that, over the period of the economic boom, suicides have increased almost in line with GDP growth, driven mainly by the deaths of males (83% of suicide victims in 2000 were male). While some of the increase may be due to better reporting, it is obvious that with economic growth there has been an increase in the numbers who feel so marginalised that they take their own life. Internationally, research has shown that suicidal behaviour is more prevalent among men, the unemployed, and those with marital problems.[6] Why the suicide rate has risen so rapidly is a topic that requires further research.

## Lessons for the Future

This chapter has examined a number of factors other than income that influence quality of life in Ireland. This and other research shows that the level of life satisfaction as expressed by individuals is not

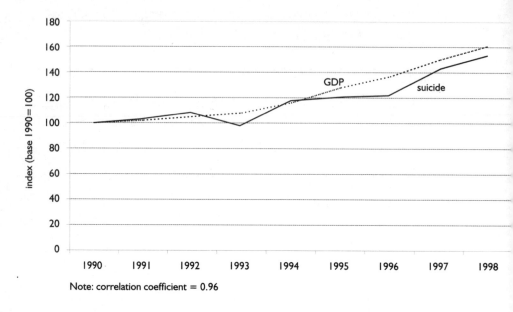

Note: correlation coefficient = 0.96

Figure 31: SUICIDES AND GDP GROWTH, 1990–1998

strongly related to GDP growth, although it is linked to the unemployment rate. Economic growth is worthwhile if for no other reason than it helps to maintain a lower rate of unemployment. People do seem to judge their satisfaction with life in terms of their expectations, or their income relative to that of others. Andrew Oswald of Warwick University has put it as follows: 'A spectator who leaps up at a football match gets at first a much better view of the game; by the time his neighbours are up it is no better than before.' Thus, the maintenance of happiness may be partly a matter of keeping up with (or even ahead of) the Joneses, but having a job is also very important.

We saw that those in the lowest socio-economic groups and those who are unemployed are considerably less satisfied with life. If a downturn in the economy results in an increase in long-term unemployment, these people will become marginalised and considerably less satisfied with life. While not examined here, it has been shown elsewhere that, all else being equal, people are also less happy when inflation is high.[7] These findings are a strong endorsement of the conventional economic wisdom that believes that low inflation and low unemployment should be the overriding goals of macro-economic policy. Maintaining full employment seems more important than maximising incomes.

However, while pursuing a stable, non-inflationary economic growth path, several other factors that influence quality of life should be addressed. In Ireland today, the problems of traffic congestion and housing provision appear to be most urgent. The high value placed by the public on their health may explain concerns regarding the quality of health services. In addition, almost a third of people suggest that the Irish have become less friendly during the economic boom as the pace of life, stress and anxiety increase. This seems to be an unfortunate side-effect of economic progress. It should serve as warning that a break-neck drive for rapid economic growth is an inappropriate goal.

Finally, while it is beyond the scope of this book and our expertise, a major effort is needed to address the most extreme expression of unhappiness with life as shown by those 300 to 400 Irish males and 80 to 90 Irish females who take their lives each year. We owe it to that most vulnerable group in society to make a huge effort to understand why, when times were thought to be so good, they felt things were so bad that they could face life no longer.

CHAPTER 13

# Envoi

*'In my end is my beginning.' T. S. Eliot*

*'The best way to predict the future is to invent it.' Unknown*

We wrote this book to explore the nature and effects of the extraordinary economic boom that Ireland experienced during the 1990s. It was originally conceived towards the end of the year 2000 as a response to then-burning questions such as: What rate of economic growth can be sustained in Ireland over the medium to longer term? Can the economy avoid a 'hard landing'? What are the appropriate policy responses to the challenges we are facing?

In the course of the year 2001 these questions – except, of course, the last – had to be recast. Even before the events of 11 September, the slowdown in the US economy had spilled over to the Irish and European economies. In Ireland, concerns about overheating were replaced by fears that slower growth could usher back the spectres of soaring unemployment and mass emigration. But some accused the Jeremiahs among academic economists of being over-pessimistic – of predicting five of the last two recessions. Business economists in Ireland and abroad, on the other hand, revealed their professional bias towards optimism in the course of 2001 by frequently stating their belief or hope that the recession would be mild and short-lived.

Indeed, they justified the riposte that they had predicted five of the last two recoveries. The truth is, to quote Yogi Berra again, 'It's tough to make predictions – especially about the future.'

The serious point is that economic shocks are, by definition, unpredictable, and historical business-cycle patterns are a poor guide to the future. At the end of the 1990s there was no way that the wisest of commentators could have anticipated the extraordinary events of 2001 – the outbreak of foot and mouth disease in Britain and its ramifications on the Irish economy, and the terrorist attacks of 11 September and their effects on the global economy. And even if some economist had had a well-functioning crystal ball that actually foresaw the second of these shocks in particular, it is a safe (if uncollectable) bet that she or he would have used this invaluable information to anticipate soaring oil prices and a prolonged stock-market collapse. In fact, neither of these repercussions materialised. One of the favourable features of the economic landscape at the end of 2001 is that oil prices rather than stock prices have collapsed – but, who knows, by the time these lines are being read another shock (escalating war in the Middle East, contagion from the Argentinean crisis, or, more probably, some as yet unforeseen crisis) could reverse these trends. And while at times like this it becomes commonplace to preface forecasts with the warning that 'we are living in extremely uncertain times', in truth, uncertainty is an enduring feature of the human condition and not just something that pops up once in a while.

Complete agnosticism is not the lesson we should draw from these reflections. While the economics soothsaying profession, like the legal profession, probably exceeds its socially optimal size, neither of them should be disbanded. Just as we need good laws and wise lawyers to interpret them, we need economists to set out the principles that should guide policy in the face of the uncertainty that is an intrinsic feature of the world in which we live. And economists *can* set out broad principles that remain valid whichever of numerous possible outcomes materialises. This is essentially what we have tried to do in this short book.

The twelve substantive chapters of the book contain our observations on the nature of the economic boom of the 1990s, its achievements and shortcomings, and the challenges facing us in the changed environment since 2000. We believe in the benefits of economic progress and indeed we have provided evidence that the Irish public by and large regards the transformation of the economy since the 1980s as a highly positive development. The reduction in unemployment from the horrendous levels of the late 1980s and early 1990s, in particular, has brought very positive social as well as economic benefits. However, we are far from believing with Dr Pangloss that not only is all well but that all is as well as could be. We devoted several chapters of the book to discussing the challenges that were not met during the boom – the failure to deal adequately with urban infrastructure, housing and roads, for example, the increasing strain that rapid economic growth has placed on amenities such as clean air and water, the continuing problems of social exclusion experienced by groups such as Travellers. And while we outlined some appropriate policy responses in these areas we acknowledge that we have not even addressed other burning issues such as the appropriate level of health care and the best way of providing it. While we do not advocate maximising economic growth as measured by GDP or some related index, we have argued strongly that all these problems could be better tackled against a backdrop of continued economic expansion.

We believe that the 1990s will, in retrospect, look like the Golden Age of modern Irish economic history, one when it was possible to combine exceptionally rapid growth in real incomes and declining unemployment with low inflation, a balance of payment surplus when the traditional fiscal constraints seemed to be non-binding so that the Minister for Finance could simultaneously cut taxes, increase expenditure *and* reduce the level of the national debt. We argued that these outcomes reflected a unique combination of favourable circumstances – the inflow of EU aid, the booming US economy and the associated surge in US investment in Ireland, the fall in real interest rates and the real exchange rate as Ireland's entry to the eurozone materialised, the rise in the proportion of the population in the economically active age group and the success of the partnership approach to wage bargaining. As we moved from the 1990s into the new millennium these favourable influences were losing their momentum. EU aid tapered off, the euro exchange rate stabilised, Irish interest rates had converged on the eurozone average, the age structure of the population was stabilising and the partnership approach to wage bargaining was becoming increasingly less appropriate in a fully-employed economy. And then the events of 2001 battered the Irish economy. During 2001 Irish wage inflation reached 10% while the exchange rate against sterling and the dollar was stable and the productivity-enhancing inflow of foreign investment slowed to a trickle. Some of these setbacks will be reversed in the medium term – although it is not possible to predict how soon – but others represent a more permanent change in the structure of the Irish economy that implies that after the current slowdown in the global economy we should not expect a return to the Golden Age. The more sombre prospect facing us now is that we are being forced to make choices once again, especially between further tax cuts and increases in publicly-provided services. One of the key messages of this book is the need realistically to face up to this more restrictive environment. In the individual chapters we have provided some guidelines as to how best to do so.

It would be inappropriate to conclude a book comprised of several short and we hope snappy treatments of individual topics with an even shorter summary of the main points. Instead, this coda is a repetition of the main principles that guided us in writing the book. These are:

➤ The importance of productivity as the long-run source of lasting gains in living standards.

➤ The role of investment in human and physical capital in raising the productivity of the labour force.

➤ The need for flexibility in response to ever-changing

circumstances and unforeseeable shocks. Nowhere is flexibility more crucial than in the labour force and its adjustment to changes in the pattern of demand.

➢ The importance of prices over centralised decision-making as the basic mechanism for allocating and reallocating economic resources.

➢ The need to reject the fear and suspicion of market forces (including the profit motive) that is a strong undercurrent in the Irish debate on public policy.

➢ Our most important message relating to fiscal policy has been the need to avoid using this policy instrument perversely, that is, to aggravate rather than alleviate economic instability, as has often occurred in the past. This implies increasing the net contribution of the tax-spending mix to aggregate demand during the current slowdown. There is a strong case for doing this by maintaining or bringing forward planned capital expenditure and no case at all for doing it by adopting a lax attitude towards public-sector pay.

➢ Environment is that part of our existence that we share, and this common-property characteristic means that the market untrammelled will not protect it. We have shown how to introduce market signals that convey scarcity and encourage the conservation of environmental endowments for ourselves and our posterity.

➢ Maintaining full employment seems more important than maximising incomes.

Adam Smith, the eighteenth-century intellectual father of modern liberal economics, pointed out that it is not to the benevolence of the baker that we owe our daily bread, but to his self-interest – his desire to make a living and feed *himself*. This view of human nature leaves many idealists dissatisfied, but it has provided an enduring insight into what makes the world go round and one that we ignore at our peril. An implication is that exhortations to altruism are likely to be less effective than getting the incentives that people face aligned with the desired outcome. There is a recurrent tendency in Irish public discourse to baulk at this philosophical orientation, a tendency that has reduced our economic performance over the years, that hindered rather than helped the realisation of the goal of attaining a fair and prosperous society. In the course of this book we have highlighted several areas where what matters is getting the incentives right rather than exhortation to be more virtuous.

But there is one area where we must still rely heavily on non-economic motivations to get things right and this is in the area of formulating and implementing public policy. Here a commitment to the common good and a careful analysis of what constitutes it are crucial. In this short book we hope we have made a contribution that will help guide policy makers in the testing time ahead.

# Glossary of Terms

**Agglomeration** Where the activities of one company or individual supports the activity of others. Thus a two-star Michelin restaurant will attract attention and clientele that is likely to benefit those restaurants and businesses in its vicinity. In general, where enterprises in the same business cluster together, they bring each other business and benefit from the specialist skills that develop in the region. Temple Bar in the tourism and culture areas and the Financial Services Centre in the area of finance were developed in part on the premise that agglomeration economies – mutual re-enforcement – will take place.

**Aggregate demand** The total level of spending on the output of the economy by domestic and foreign consumers and investors, and by government.

**Alternative energy** Conventionally, energy is supplied by burning fossil fuels, including coal, oil, natural gas, peat, and by nuclear power. Alternative energy sources are those not included in this conventional basket, including energy from wind, wave, biomass and solar, which are renewable.

**Automatic stabilisers** When an economy goes into recession, more people are unemployed. They receive unemployment benefits, and government automatically increases its outlays. At the same time, government receipts from income tax, VAT, excise and other taxes, fall off. The increase in expenditure and reduction in tax revenue helps reduce the intensity of the recession and stabilise the economy. See 'Multiplier'.

**Baby boom** The 'boomers' in the US are that generation that were born after the Second World War, when returning soldiers settled down and had relatively large families. In Ireland, the improved economic circumstances in the 1960s and 1970s combined with other factors to produce the Irish equivalent.

**Carbon monoxide (CO)** This is produced when coal, oil, gas, peat are burned. It is colourless, odourless, and non-irritating, but can be fatal when ingested in confined ill-ventilated spaces, e.g. indoors.

**CFCs** Chlorofluorocarbons are synthetic compounds introduced in the 1930s by the Du Pont and General Motors Corporations as refrigerants. They are inert, odourless, colourless and non-toxic. They enabled refrigerators to become household commodities, and had a major influence in facilitating the economic and social development of regions such as the southern US and warmer regions of the world generally. But scientists in 1974 indicated that they may be depleting the ozone layer in the atmosphere, which absorbs ultraviolet light; if we receive too much ultraviolet light, the likelihood of our getting skin cancer and other ailments such as snow blindness, cataracts and advanced ageing of the skin is significantly increased. The 'ozone hole' was discovered by the British Antarctic survey in 1985, proving that ozone depletion was a fact, and this led to the banning of CFCs.

**Clean development mechanism (CDM)** This is a 'flexible mechanism' provided for in the Kyoto Protocol to the Climate Change Convention. It allows companies and others in developed countries to invest in projects in developing countries that reduce greenhouse gas emissions, and to claim these emissions reductions as a contribution to meeting their quota.

**Demand-side measures** In macroeconomics, efforts to stablise the level of economic activity by policy interventions that affect the level of *aggregate demand*. At the microeconomic level, efforts to change the volume and pattern of consumer demand such as, in the case of traffic, incentives to commuters to take collective transport, the use of parking charges to influence the location, timing and volume of car use, electronic road pricing

**Directive (European)** A Directive (of the European Union) has to be implemented in the member states. It is usually transposed into the domestic law of each member state. Non compliance can result in the Commission taking the country in question before the European Court. Convictions can result in very substantial fines.

**Economically inactive** A person who is neither working nor looking for work outside the home is described as 'economically inactive'. They could be retired, independently wealthy or, more usually, engaged in 'household production' – that is rearing a family and managing a household.

**Efficiency (economic)** Two types of economic efficiency are recognised. 'Static' efficiency means getting the most out of the resources that are being applied to achieve a particular objective. This is also often associated with 'cost-effectiveness' or achieving a target at least cost. 'Dynamic efficiency' is about creating a context where creativity and innovation are encouraged and facilitated, so that performance is optimised over time.

**Elastic labour supply** Means that the number at work in the economy – and individual sectors and regions – expands and contracts readily at prevailing wages.

**Emissions trading** Individual entities – usually companies – are assigned a quota for their emissions of a specified pollutant that they may not exceed per unit time, usually a year. But they may buy or sell quota, so long as they hold sufficient permits to 'cover' their emissions. Out of these transactions comes a price per unit of emissions. This price signals to polluters that it is worth their while reducing their emissions as long as the cost of such reduction is less than what they can get in the market place for the part of their emissions quota that they can sell as a result of such reduction. It is a 'flexible mechanism' in the Kyoto Protocol to the Climate Change Convention and it is envisaged that trades will be able to take place across national frontiers.

**Environmental economics** That branch of economics that addresses choices as regards how our environmental endowments are used. It involves examining how to mobilise markets to achieve the integration of development and environmental objectives and the assessment of benefits and costs of alternatives. It is regarded by many as amongst the noblest of the economic fields.

**Expansionary budget** When a government borrows money to finance some of its expenditure, this tends to expand the overall level of economic activity on the basis that money is taken mainly from savers, and transferred to those who spend it on goods and services. This increases *aggregate demand* and leads to an expansion in output. And those who receive the 'first round' of such expenditure themselves spend part of it on more goods and services, and so on. To the extent that some of such government expenditure is spent on imports and/or is saved, the expansionary effect is diminished. Because of the 'leakage' to imports, using deficit financing to stimulate activity in a small open economy (with a high level of imports) can only be a very short-term solution to the problem of a faltering economy. See 'Stimulus to demand'.

**External factors** Those things that affect us, such as the weather, over which we individually have little or no control. Not to be confused with *externalities*.

**Externalities** These occur when one firm or consumer's activities affect other firms or consumers. If I keep my garden attractive, my neighbour benefits – this is a positive externality. If a farmer pollutes a river, there is a negative externality for anglers. These effects are also known as *spillovers*.

**Fiscal policy** Where government manipulates the total level of public taxation and expenditure to influence the level of economic activity.

**Flexible mechanisms** These are provided for in the Kyoto Protocol to the Climate Change Convention. They are: emissions trading, the clean development mechanism (CDM) and joint implementation (JI). The flexibility comes from the fact that all three allow the company or other entity to meet part of all of its greenhouse gas emissions quota by paying some other entity to achieve reductions on their behalf.

**Free riders** Those who benefit from an action without incurring any of the costs. When your residents' association has a 'clean-up' day in your estate in which you do not participate but whose benefits you enjoy, you are a 'free rider'.

**Full employment** When the unemployment rate drops so low that any further reduction would tend to spark off a 'wage explosion'. There is no agreement as to what unemployment rate constitutes full employment, but in Irish conditions it lies in the region of 4%.

**Global recession** Ireland sells a high proportion of its output to other countries, notably the UK, the US and the EU. When those economies go into recession, they purchase less from abroad, and this adversely affects our economy. When the 'big three' – Europe, the US and Japan – simultaneously go into recession, then there is global recession.

**Global warming** The planet is made habitable by greenhouse gasses in the atmosphere. These act as sort of blanket that retains for us some of the heat from the sun that is reflected back from the earth. Carbon dioxide is an important greenhouse gas. When coal, oil, gas or peat are burned the carbon is released; it combines with oxygen to comprise carbon dioxide ($CO_2$). For well over a century we have been adding such large quantities of carbon dioxide and other greenhouse gasses to the atmosphere that many have concluded we are warming the globe.

**Globalisation** The process whereby goods, services and ideas spreads throughout the world – a McDonald's on every street corner, a Starbucks on every block, a coke in every hand, the Simpsons on every TV and democracy in every country – associated with free flows of capital and of labour in some regions such as the European Union. Globalisation also implies mobility of labour – a growing flow of migrants between countries.

**Gross Domestic Product (GDP)** The value of goods and services produced in an economy, usually expressed on an annual basis. In some minds, this has become synonymous with well-being. On its own, in fact, it tells us little about how we are doing, any more than we can judge a company on the basis of the level of its output of goods and services. Numerous companies with turnover in billions go out of business every year. But many features we do value, such as rising disposable income, ability of government to increase expenditure without raising tax rates, increasing employment, are associated with rising real GDP. Rapid growth in GDP is associated with other less attractive features of life, including more traffic congestion, rapid increases in the cost of accommodation, and increases in some forms of pollution. Closely related to the concept of national income.

**Gross National Product (GNP)** The same as GDP except for the addition of net-factor income from abroad. These are the flows of payments to labour and capital into and out of the country. In Ireland there is an exceptionally large net outflow under this heading due to the profits of the foreign-owned companies that operate here. In Ireland, GDP exceeds GNP by over 15%, whereas in most countries the gap is negligible.

**Groundwater** The water stored beneath the surface, in what is termed an 'aquifer'. Over time, much of this store makes its way to rivers and the sea, and is renewed by precipitation. It is used extensively in the countryside as the primary source of water for domestic and animal use and in some cases by industry. It can be contaminated by bacteria and hazardous materials that leak ('leach') into the store of water, creating problems for those using it.

**Income distribution** This refers to the way national income or GDP is distributed between income groups. Included here are the issues of inequality and poverty. It is concerned with the question of Who gets what or How the national cake is divided up.

**Inflation** Every month, the Central Statistics Office collects prices on a basket of goods thought to be representative of consumer purchases. The rate of price rise in this basket comprises the rate of inflation in consumer prices. This is usually indexed to a base year, and is called the Consumer Price Index (CPI). The CPI in August 2001 to base year November 1975=100 was 532.5, which tells us that consumer prices rose by 5.325 times between 1975 and 2001, i.e. we would need €5.325 in 2001 to buy the same basket of goods as the equivalent of €1 would have purchased in 1975. Such indices are also compiled for wholesale goods, wages etc..

**Joint implementation (JI)** This is a 'flexible mechanism' provided for in the Kyoto Protocol to the Climate Change Convention. It allows companies and others in developed countries to invest in projects in other developed countries that reduce greenhouse gas emissions, and to claim these emissions reductions as a contribution to meeting their quota. It is envisaged that most of such investment would be made by the OECD member countries in countries of the former Eastern block and Soviet Union.

**Keynesian model** John Maynard Keynes was the most eminent economist of the twentieth century. Among his many contributions is his model that argues that when a country is in recession or depression, one solution is for government to 'prime' the economy by deficit spending, or by injecting new purchasing power into the system. The multiplier effect of such new purchasing power will restore the economy to health. The corollary is that when an economy is booming, government should take money out of the economy to slow it down, and to correct the fiscal imbalances resulting from deficit spending.

**Kyoto Protocol** The UN conference on Environment and Development in Rio de Janeiro in 1992 agreed the Framework Convention on Climate Change. The signatories agreed in this convention to stabilise emissions of greenhouse gasses, but without specifying how or by whom this would be done. The Kyoto Protocol to this convention was agreed in the Japanese city of the same name in 1997, in which the industrialised countries agreed to quantitative limits on their emissions, using their emissions in 1990 as the base year.

**Labour force** The people available to work in an economy. The size will depend on a number of factors, including how attractive and easy it is for women working in the home to work outside in the economy, the numbers graduating from the educational system, the numbers living abroad willing to work in Ireland.

**Lags** When the government increases spending or cuts taxes to stimulate the economy, it may be some time before these measures take effect. There is a lag between the policy response and its impact on the economy.

**Macroeconomy** Typically describes characteristics that apply to a national economy, including Gross Domestic Product (GDP), total disposable income, rates of price and wage inflation, total employment and rate of unemployment etc. Macroeconomics focuses on how to manage a national economy so as to achieve overall performance objectives. See 'Gross Domestic Product (GDP)'.

**Marrakech agreement** In Marrakech in November 2001, agreement was reached by the parties to the Kyoto Protocol to the Climate Change Convention on the rules that would apply in implementing the terms of the Protocol, including the 'flexible mechanisms,' monitoring and enforcement, and carbon sequestration (whereby carbon is stored by trees and other plant life).

**Modal split** The share of trips using various forms of transport. Over time, in most cities, including Ireland's, the modal split shows an increasing share taken by the individual in a car, as opposed to cycling, bus, train, tram and walking.

**Monetary policy** Monetary policy involves changes in the money supply or more usually in interest rates. For example, the US Federal Reserve Bank – its Central Bank – aggressively lowered interest rates in the course of 2001 to try to avert recession. Ireland and the other members of the euro group have ceded this power to the European Central Bank in Frankfurt, which now sets a 'one size fits all' monetary policy for the thirteen euro-zone member states.

**Multinational company or enterprise (MNC or MNE)** Firms that operate on a global basis. This is true of most of the world's leading companies today – from the big pharmaceutical and computer companies to the largest banks to producers of consumer goods such as McDonald's food, Nike sportswear and Coke.

**Multiplier** A relevant illustration of this idea is provided by an increase in tourism in a country like Ireland. When 'additional expenditure' by visitors to Ireland is spent on goods and services, those receiving the money spend part of it on more goods and services, then those receiving this money also spend part of it on goods and services, and so on through continuing rounds. At each round, the effect gets weaker because some of the money received is saved and some is spent on imports. The GDP multiplier for tourism expenditure in Ireland is approximately one. Thus an additional €100 million of tourist expenditure adds the same to our GDP. Of course, this can happen only if there are unemployed resources (hotels, staff etc.) available to the sector. A danger with the concept is that it can used to bolster the case for certain projects, such as the proposed new Dublin sports complex, when, in fact, it is not a special attribute of that project. If the same money were spent, say, on a casino, this would have much the same multiplier effect.

**National income** See GDP.

**Nitrogen oxides (NOx)** Refers to nitrogen oxide (NO) and nitrogen dioxide ($NO_2$). The latter is a reddish brown gas with a pungent odour. It contributes to the 'browning' and odour of polluted cities. It is relatively insoluble, and can pass through the nose and mouth, to lodge in the lungs, with damaging effects on health. It also combines with water to produce nitric acid, resulting in 'acid rain' that adversely affects productivity of crops and corrosion of materials. Photochemical smog is produced by the interaction of nitrogen oxides and sunlight.

**Nominal** In economics, this refers to money amount as contrasted with purchasing power. Thus, nominal wages could be increasing at a rate of 10% per year, but if price inflation is averaging 12% annually, wages net of inflation are falling. See 'Inflation' and 'Real'.

**One-off housing** Used to describe a house built on its own site rather than being clustered with others. Because many such houses in the countryside are one-storey bungalows, this phenomenon has been popularised as 'bungalow blitz', 'bungalow blight', or 'bungalow bliss', depending on the predilection of the commentator.

**Openness (of economy)** The extent to which an economy trades with the rest of the world. One way to measure openness is to add exports to imports, and divide this total by Gross Domestic Product for that year, expressed as a percentage. On this basis, Ireland's openness has risen from about 50% in 1960 to close to 200% in 2002.

**Opportunity cost** What is being foregone by taking one action rather than another. The opportunity cost of spending three hours visiting your mother is an evening's drinking in your local pub.

**Overheating (economy)** Where demand for goods and services is outstripping the ability to supply to the extent that prices – of labour, services, housing etc. – start to rise rapidly to bring demand and supply into balance.

**Oxidised** A process whereby elements combine with oxygen to create new substances. Thus, when an element such as sulphur or nitrogen is released into the atmosphere it combines with the oxygen there to make sulphur and nitrogen oxides.

**Particulate Matter** This is released into the atmosphere when incomplete combustion takes place. When the particulates are very small, they can be particularly lethal to human health, as they move through nose and mouth to lodge in the lungs. Older people whose respiratory system has been weakened, and young babies whose system is not fully developed, are particularly vulnerable.

**Pro-cyclical budget** Where an economy is already booming due to external factors, and domestic policies intensify the boom.

**Productivity** Output per unit of input. In economics, usually refers to real output per person employed, but a more sophisticated measure called 'Total Factor Productivity' measures output per unit of combined capital and labour.

**Real** 'Real' is used to signify that the effects of inflation have been netted out. 'Nominal' is where such effects have not been taken out. When we say that Ireland's real GDP rose by over 8% per year in the 1990s, we mean that the effects of inflation have already been deducted from this figure. The nominal rate of growth exceeded this by the rate of inflation. If we say that a price has risen in real terms this means it has risen at a rate greater than the inflation rate. See 'Inflation' and 'Nominal'.

**Regional policy** The means whereby a particular country or continent's space is divided up and governed, where governance includes decisions on the allocation of resources. Some European countries, such as Spain, Germany and Belgium, have regions defined largely by history, culture and in some cases linguistic distinctiveness, that have their own regional parliaments and substantial powers. In other countries, including Ireland, regions are defined mainly on the basis of socio-economic characteristics, and regional policy focuses on the most deprived regions with the objective of 'bridging the gap' between the richer and poorer, typically with the delegation of little if any autonomous powers.

**Social housing** Housing where the State takes a hand in helping meet the accommodation needs of particular individuals and groups. Traditionally associated with the provision of public housing in estates or flat complexes, the menu has expanded to include voluntary housing associations and other groups who gain assistance via various mechanisms including provision of sites, grants and loans.

**Spillovers** See 'Externalities'.

**Sulphur dioxide (SO₂)** A relatively soluble gas produced when sulphur-bearing substances like coal and oil are burned and release the element to air. It produces dry mouth, scratchy throat and smarting eyes. It also combines with water to produce sulphuric acid, resulting in 'acid rain', which adversely affects productivity of crops and corrosion of materials.

**Sunk costs** Costs already incurred. The ability to ignore sunk costs in making decisions about the future is a pre-requisite for success in business.

**Tight labour market** As the economy approaches 'full employment' there is a high level of demand for labour relative to the supply, and real wages tend to rise rapidly. The following sign in a Dublin restaurant: 'Help wanted immediately: ability to speak English an advantage' is an indication of a tightening labour market.

**Tonnes of Oil Equivalent (TOE)** Energy comes from a wide range of sources, including natural gas, wood, coal, peat, oil, wind. In order to compare the amounts of energy coming from different sources, it is necessary to be able to express them in common terms, and 'oil equivalent' has emerged as the means for doing this. One TOE is approximately equivalent in energy content terms to 2.257 tonnes of peat briquettes, 1.504 tonnes of coal, and 1235 cubic metres of natural gas (Kinsale field).

**Transactions costs** The costs of transacting business. The time and money involved in doing title searches, getting planning permission, getting a loan, complying with building regulations etc. are some of the transactions costs involved in buying or modifying a house. It can also apply to the costs involved in getting a group to reach a decision.

**Unemployment** An unemployed person is one who is not working but actively looking for work. See 'economically inactive'.

**Visual loss** The loss of something that was pleasing to the eye, such as a country scene or a beautiful building. Visual sensibility is related to understanding. Constable observed: 'You can't see what you don't understand.'

**Wage flexibility** Where wages move up and down in response to changes in the market place. Thus, in late 2001 workers in a number of IT companies took a 10% cut in nominal wages – close to 15% in real terms – to help secure the future of the company in recessionary times. In some sectors wage flexibility has increased due to the growing importance of bonuses and other extra payments that be scaled back during bad times and increased in good times.

# Notes

## Preface

1   Mitroff, Ian, and Anagnos, Gus, *Managing Crises Before They Happen*, Amacom, 2001, cited in *Financial Times*, 26 September 2001, p.14.

2   11th Annual R&D Scoreboard, Department of Trade and Industry, London, 2001, reported in *Financial Times*, 27 September 2001, p.14.

## Chapter 2 The Boom and Its Aftermath

1   Mjøset, Lars, *The Irish Economy in a Comparative Institutional Perspective*, National Economic and Social Council Report No. 93, Dublin, 1992.

2   For surveys see Walsh, Brendan, 'From Rags to Riches: Ireland's Economic Boom', *World Economics*, October–December 2000, and Economic and Social Research Institute *Medium Term Review 2001-2007*, ESRI, Dublin, September 2001.

3   Keating, William, 'Measuring the Economy: Problems and Prospects', paper read to the Statistical and Social Inquiry Society of Ireland, 26 October 2000.

4   Madden, David, and Smith, Fiona, 'Poverty in Ireland, 1987-1994: A Stochastic Dominance Approach', *Economic and Social Review*, 31 (3), July 2001, pp.187-214.

5   There is a difference here between European and US practice – reliance on absolute poverty measures is more usual in the US, while many in Europe favour relative poverty measures.

6    A slightly different picture emerges from alternative ways of constructing the income scale.

7    Gropp, R., and Kostial, K., 'The Disappearing Tax Base: Is Foreign Direct Investment Eroding Corporate Income Taxes?', European Central Bank, Working Paper No. 31, 2000, p. 19.

8    European Directorate-General for Research, 'The Reform of Taxation in EU Member States', *Economic Affairs Series, Econ 127 EN*, Luxembourg, 2001.

## Chapter 3 The Importance of Productivity

1    A further refinement is to express output per hour worked, since being able to produce the same output in fewer hours implies more leisure, which is a gain.

2    We use Gross *National* Product (GNP) rather than Gross *Domestic* Product (GDP) to measure the economy's growth because it is a better guide to the trend in living standards. A further downward adjustment to the growth rate is required to take account of the deterioration in the terms of trade as the euro weakened. With a weaker currency, for a given amount of cash, we can buy less imports from those countries with stronger currencies.

3    A point to bear in mind is that much more of the employment growth in the Netherlands was part-time than was the case in Ireland.

4    'Elastic' meaning that as more labour is required, it is readily forthcoming.

## Chapter 4 Globalisation: The Faustian Bargain

1    The fact that the openness grew more rapidly in constant prices than in current prices reflects the tendency for the relative price of imports and especially exports to decline over time.

2    These points are developed in 'Globalisation and its critics', *The Economist*, 29 September 2001.

3    Before Ireland joined the EU, our agriculture competed effectively in the global market place, without benefit of price supports or protection.

## Chapter 5 Population and Immigration

1    A point to bear in mind is that much more of the employment growth in the Netherlands was part-time than was the case in Ireland.

2    For the source see Meenan, James, in *The Irish Economy since 1922*, Liverpool University Press, 1970, p. 332.

3    Barry, Frank, Murphy, Anthony, Strobl, Eric, and Walsh, Brendan, 'A Review of the Economic Appraisal System for Projects Seeking Support from the Industrial Development Agencies', Workshop Paper, University Industry Centre, University College Dublin, 9 November 2000.

4    The impact of a brain drain on the countries from which the immigrants come should also be taken into account.

## Chapter 6 Economic Policy Responses

1    Duffy, D., et al, 'Medium-term Review 2001-2007', Economic and Social Research Institute, Dublin, September 2001.

2    See MacCoille, Conall, and McCoy, Daniel, 'Smoothening Adjustment through Modified Wage Bargaining', Dublin Economics Workshop, October 2001.

## Chapter 7 Spatial Strategy

1    See Connellan, Liam, 'A framework for Ireland's future spatial strategy', Proceedings of Institution of Engineers in Ireland, Annual Conference 2001.

## Chapter 8 Accommodation

1    From Bacon, Peter, and Associates, in association with MacCabe, Fergal, *The Housing Market in Ireland: an Economic Evaluation of Trends and Prospects*, June 2000. This report provides a detailed analysis of housing market trends, potential house supply, econometric analysis of the housing market and projections, assessment of government actions on the housing market, and a series of appendices addressing significant areas of undeveloped land in the greater Dublin area, and the status of the service land initiative.

2       McCoy, Daniel, Duffy, David, Hore, Jonathan, and MacCoille, Conall, *Quarterly Economic Commentary*, Economic and Social Research Institute, Dublin, October 2001, p. 77.

3       Section 23 of the Finance Act allowed the investor in rental property to set off the cost of the building against rental income for tax purposes.

4       Assuming an average site value of €50,000, and average agricultural land value of €5,000, yielding an average capital gain of €45,000, applied to the 18,000 one-off houses built annually.

5       Sixteen such areas have been identified – mainly on the western seaboard and the north midlands – by government for special treatment under an initiative called Ceantair Laga Ard-Riachtanais (CLAR). Reported in *The Irish Times*, 6 October 2001, p. 3.

6       So called because the idea was first formalised by Garret Hardin in his article 'The Tragedy of the Commons', *Science*, 69, 1978.

## Chapter 9 Traffic Congestion

1       See Clinch, J.P., 'Reconciling Rapid Economic Growth and Environmental Sustainability in Ireland', Barrington Lecture, *Journal of the Statistical and Social Inquiry Society of Ireland*, forthcoming 2002.

2       Much of the rest of this paper is adapted from Clinch, J.P., and Kelly, J.A., 'Economics of Traffic Congestion in Dublin', *Environmental Studies Research Series, ESRS 01/09*, Department of Environmental Studies, University College Dublin, 2001.

## Chapter 10 Environment

1       Much of the data in this chapter are taken from: Stapleton, L., Lehane, M., and Toner, P., *Ireland's Environment: a Millennium Report*, Environmental Protection Agency, Wexford, 2000.

2       The material in this section draws heavily on: Clinch, J. Peter, and McLoughlin, Eoin, 'A Preliminary Analysis of the Ban on Bituminous Coal in Dublin', *Environmental Studies Research Series, ESRS 01/08*, Department of Environmental Studies, University College Dublin, 2001.

3       Clinch, J. Peter, 'The Environmental Performance of Industry', paper presented at the Achievement and Challenge conference, University College Dublin, 10-14 September 2001.

4       Stapleton et al. (*ibid.*).

5       Much of the data and insight in this section is drawn from: Barry, Conor P., and Convery, Frank J., 'The Applicability and Policy Relevance of Environmental Protection Expenditure Accounting', *Environmental Studies Research Series, ESRS 01/04*, Department of Environmental Studies, University College Dublin, 2001.

6       The proposed introduction of a tax on plastic bags is a small but symbolically important effort to express in the market place the desirability to re-use and recycle. However, it will work only if there are clear, efficient and unambiguous implementing mechanisms in place to make it work.

7       The UCD Department of Environmental Studies is co-ordinating the European research network on emissions trading, and via a rolling series of workshops and publications providing the latest findings and practices in this emerging field. See www.emissionstradingnetwork.com.

## Chapter 11 Climate Change and Energy

1       Fossil fuels include coal, natural gas and oil. They are so called because they are made of living matter which millions of years ago accumulated on the planet. Carbon is a key element in their composition, and when such fuel is burned, the carbon is released and combines with oxygen in the atmosphere to comprise carbon dioxide ($CO$). Peat, which was formed since the last Ice Age, and is thus much more recent in origin, is also carbon based, while trees and plant life are similarly organic in character and release their carbon to the atmosphere when burned.

2       Bert Bolin headed the team of scientists mobilised by the Intergovernmental Panel on Climate Change (IPCC) to advise on climate change. In Bolin, Bert, 'Key features of the global climate system to be considered in analysis of the climate change issue', *Environment and Development Economics*, Vol.3 (3), July 1998, pp. 348-365, he summarises some of the issues and impacts.

3    A more catastrophic outcome for Europe would be a violent change in the North Atlantic Drift ('Gulf Stream') that diminished its emollient effects on the climate of Northern Europe. According to Knut Alfsen, this is 'something which is not expected, but may not be totally disregarded'.

4    All of the data in what follows is taken from: Duffy, David, Fitz Gerald, John, Hore, Jonathan, Kearney, Ide, and MacCoille, Conall, *Medium Term Review, 2001-2007*, No. 8., ESRI, Dublin, 2001, pp. ix, 85, 86, 88. This Medium Term Review is part of a rolling sequence published by the ESRI led by John Fitz Gerald that provides the most consistent, comprehensive and insightful view of emerging trends and prospects for the Irish economy. It integrates economic trends at global and EU levels with national macro, sectoral and environmental performance in Ireland.

5    O'Rourke, Kevin, 'Energy Trends, Challenges, Prospects,' paper presented at the Rio + 10 Achievement and Challenge Conference, UCD, Dublin, September 2001,  pp.10-14.

6    Defined in this instance as not being able to produce electricity as cheaply as the least cost alternative generating source.

## Chapter 12 Quality of Life

1    Quoted by Oswald, A.J., 'Happiness and Economic Performance', *Economic Journal,* 107, 1997, pp.1815-31.

2    A simple analysis is presented here but more detailed technical papers are available from the authors.

3    Source: Eurobarometer, 'Report Number 54', European Commission, Brussels, 2001.

4    Derived from Oswald (*ibid.*) and Eurobarometer (*ibid.*).

5    Oswald (*ibid*).

6    Oswald (*ibid.*).

7    See DiTella, R., MacCulloch, R.J., and Oswald, A.J, 'Preferences over Inflation and Unemployment: Evidence from Surveys of Happiness', *American Economic Review*, 91, 2001, pp.335-41.

# Index

free riders 115, 121
frugality 20
fuel poverty, and energy conservation 137

**G**

gas, natural 155, 157
gateway centres 100-1
GDP 25, 39, 40, 57
    compared to turnover of large corporations 62
    and employment 85-6
    growth 25, 27, 30
    per person 43-4, 80
    and population 79-80
    and public policy 69
    and traffic congestion 127
General Motors 54
*General Theory of Population* 73
Germany 168
    energy-efficient housing 113
global warming 146-50
    plan of action 152
globalisation 53-67
    and democratic deficit 64
    of environmental concerns 146
    and erosion of national economic sovereignty 62-3
    lessons for the future 65-7
    as positive force 66-7
    protests against 53-4, 59, 63, 65-6
    risks 65
    unfairness to poorer countries 65-7
    world index of 58
GNP 45
gombeenism 19, 135
Gomez, Lefty 89
Greece 28, 167
greenhouse gases 132, 146-50, 153-4, 163
groundwater, in single-house development 106
growth
    intensive and extensive 44-50
    output and productivity 44
    sources of 45
    sustainability 85
growth in GDP and vehicle numbers 119
growth rate of Irish economy 25-6
*GSI Groundwater Newsletter, The* 106

**H**

Hague, The 151
happiness, factors influencing 169-71
harder times, preparing for 36-9
Hardin, Garrett 121
Hartley, L.P. 171
health 173-4, 177, 180
High Frequency Economics 37
Hiroshima 136
Home Energy Management 160
*Homes for the 21st Century* 137
house prices, and public transport 99
household income, rise in 31
housing 52, 102-16, 177
    energy-efficient 113, 160
    house prices 73, 99, 102-3
    incentives for cluster development 112-13
    lessons for the future 111-16
    one-off 105-7, 112, 113, 135
    social 103-4
    and tax incentives 104
    and transport 107, 121, 139-40
    *see also* accommodation

**I**

IDA (Industrial Development Agency) 29
Illich, Ivan 18
immigration 27, 47, 68-82, 74
    asylum seekers 80, 103
    benefits 71, 78
    and labour force 76-7
    need for coherent approach 79
    and population 68-82
    public attitudes to immigrants 77-8
    and racism 68, 79
    in West Cork 80
income distribution, and fairness 23
income tax *see* taxation
India 73
industrial peace 29
inflation 60, 83-5, 176-7
    hidden 74
    in housing market 78
    and oil prices 37
    wage 91-2, 94, 181
information 22
information technology 30, 40, 49, 81
infrastructure
    improvements 39
    investment in 101
    and one-off housing 105-7, 113
    transport 127-8
innovation 21-2, 51
insurance, car 129
Integrated Pollution Control Licensing 142
interest rates 83, 86
Intergovernmental Panel on Climate Change 149
*International Herald Tribune* 37, 64, 165
*International Journal for Housing Science* 137
International Monetary Fund 63
investment in human and physical capital 181
Irish economy, openness of 56
Irish Energy Centre 155-7, 160, 163
    self-audit scheme 156
*Irish Times, The* 66, 158
Irvine, Andy 24
Italy 28